I0844429

Forty Stories of Error

DELVIS ECHEVERRIA

Copyright © 2024 Delvis Echeverria

All rights reserved.

ISBN: 9798868155857

DEDICATION

To my dearest abuela Cuca,

This book is a humble tribute to you, the driving force behind many of my stories and achievements. Your unwavering love and support have propelled me to pursue my dreams and my freedom with passion and determination.
And without aiming to politicize this dedication, soon, very soon, when Cuba is free, we will recover your coffee farms and the freedom that has been taken from us for over 65 years.

CONTENTS

ACKNOWLEDGMENTS

I would like to express my sincere gratitude to all those friends and colleagues who have taken the time to provide feedback on this book. Your valuable comments and contributions have been essential in the creation and refinement of this work. Your support and dedication have been invaluable, and I am deeply thankful for your generosity in sharing your ideas and perspectives. Thank you for contributing your knowledge and for being a crucial part in bringing this project to fruition.

Ariannis Abella, Abhishek Rai, Meiby Yeras, Violena Hernández, Miguel Buitrago, Christopher Valenciano, Federico Toledo, Nadia Cavalleri, Leandro Meléndez, Priya Ahluwalia, Angel Lambert, Diego Leiva; and Mario Martin Fabrizio for his exceptional artistic vision and dedication in bringing captivating illustrations.

FOREWORD

Welcome to a fascinating journey through the history of software errors and the flaws that have shaped our digital age. In these pages, we will discover how small mistakes have significantly impacted our economy, politics, and even the loss of human lives. But before we delve into this world of failures and bugs, allow me to share my own story.

Without intending to politicize or polarize, I aim to share my story and perspective on freedom when it comes to writing. I don't seek to offend anyone or influence others' thoughts; rather, this is my personal perspective as a human being and professional.

For many, expressing themselves or even writing what they desire might not seem extraordinary. In my case (like many Cubans born and raised in Cuba) the freedom to exist as a human holds immeasurable value. It is straightforward for others to undervalue something as natural as being able to think and write freely. I grew up under a government's rules that controlled what was written and published and held ownership over everything, including schools and universities.

They exercised control over what to do, how to do it, and even what topics you could address in your writing. Furthermore, they appropriated research, presentations, and conferences, distributing them solely among politically aligned individuals. Writing and conducting research on any topic were only possible under the watchful eye of leaders and organizations aligned with the government. These obstacles, along with others, particularly those rooted in political matters, served as catalysts that urged me to leave my homeland.

As a Cuban immigrant I discovered a newfound sense of liberation that allowed me to pursue my passions unhindered. The freedom to express myself became the cornerstone of my writing journey. It is with a profound sense of gratitude and unwavering determination that I embark on this endeavor, seeking to contribute to the body of knowledge, enrich the understanding of our technological past, and ignite discussions that transcend borders. Through this book, I also aspire to honor the freedom I have found.

Now, I am living in the Sunshine State in Southwest Florida – a beautiful region located on the Gulf Coast. With its many nationally protected areas and wide variety of beaches, this area is a real paradise. Among the area's many great cities – Naples, Marco Island, Cape Coral, Bonita Spring, Sanibel, and Punta Gorda, among others – I have found that one of them has a particularly rich and interesting history: the city of Fort Myers. As a resident of Southwest Florida, I have immersed myself in the history of this region, delving into the life of Thomas Edison, who spent many winters in Fort Myers. I have invested time in visiting local museums and reading books, old newspapers, and historical letters. During this process of discovery, I came across interesting facts about Edison that I had never heard before. To my surprise, I found that Thomas Edison often used a term that is now commonly employed by software developers, coders, software engineers, and QA testers in the software industry: bug.

In today's computer world, the word bug describes an error in a software program. This finding piqued my curiosity and spurred me to investigate further. How and when did the use of this term originate? Are there records predating Edison that reveal its use in a similar context? With these questions in mind, I embarked on a rigorous systematic literature review to uncover the origins of this interesting word and its evolution throughout history.

In the following pages, I will share with you the fruits of this research, presenting historical evidence that supports the use of the term "bug" since the 19th Century. Additionally, I will share 40 stories of software errors that have left indelible marks on our society, often going unnoticed despite their significant consequences. Through a simple and straightforward writing style, my aim is for this work to be accessible and understandable to all readers.

Software errors reflect our own humanity and alongside the relentless pursuit of technological perfection. From economic failures to political crises, from the loss of human lives to the birth of revolutionary innovations, the events of each story will teach us valuable lessons about the challenges we face in the digital age.

So, I invite you to embark on this journey with me, to explore the forgotten past of software errors, and to gain a better understanding of our technological present and future. Within these pages, I aim to ignite a shared passion for history and technology, as we uncover the pivotal errors that have shaped our world. Join me on this captivating journey delving into the history of software bugs through 40 enthralling stories that redefine our technological narrative.

Chapter 1:

THE HISTORY BEHIND THE TERM BUG

14

Thomas Edison and the term "Bug".

Thomas Edison is a name that is synonymous with innovation, creativity, and invention. Over the course of his long and distinguished career, Edison made countless contributions to the field of technology, from the incandescent light bulb to the phonograph. But few people realize that Edison also had a special connection to Fort Myers, Florida, where he spent many winters and completed some of his most important work.

In 1885, Thomas Alva Edison was traveling along Florida's west coast and stopped to visit Fort Myers. Enjoying his time there, he soon bought 13 acres along the Caloosahatchee River and built a winter home he named Seminole Lodge. During his winters in Fort Myers, Edison was prolific in his work, using his time there to develop many of his most important inventions. In 1887, for example, Edison invented the phonograph, a device that would revolutionize the music industry and pave the way for modern recording technology. Edison also experimented with electric power and lighting, and he spent countless hours in his laboratory at Seminole Lodge, tinkering with new ideas and designs.

In addition to his inventing work, Edison was also a fixture in the community of Fort Myers. He was known for his love of nature and his dedication to preserving the natural beauty of the area. He was instrumental in establishing the Edison and Ford Winter Estates, which are now popular tourist attractions and a testament to Edison's love of the area.[1]

Many people think the term bug was coined by the computer programmer Grace Hopper in the 1940s. However, my research into Fort Myers revealed that, more than sixty years earlier, Thomas Edison used the term to describe technical problems that occur during the process of innovation.

In his 1876 notes on his lighting inventions, one of his entries reads,

"Awful lot of bugs still." [2]

Two years later, Edison wrote two letters to Western Union President, William Orton:

"You were partly correct, I did find a 'bug' in my apparatus, but it was not in the telephone proper. It was of the genus 'callbellum.' The insect appears to find conditions for its existence in all call apparatus of telephones." [3]

And, in a letter to Theodore Puskás, he wrote:

"This thing gives out and then that. 'Bug' — as such little faults and difficulties are called — show themselves, and months of anxious watching, study, and labor are requisite before commercial success — or failure — is certainly reached." [4]

In a 1916 article on Edison's team of researchers (his "Insomnia Squad"), a reporter notes that they worked "like fiends when they were 'fishing for a bug.' That means that they are searching for some missing quality, quantity, or combination that will add something toward the perfect whole."

Decoding "Bug": Edison's Role in Technological Terminology.

Thomas Edison has often been credited with coining the term "bug" in a technological context. As mentioned in previous pages, the term itself first appeared in 1876, where in one of his notes regarding an invention, it reads, "Awful lot of bugs still." However, after a thorough analysis of references, based on notes, patents, and books about Edison, there is evidence that Edison had used the term before 1876. Furthermore, others were also using the term within the technological jargon of that era.

During the year 1873, Edison dedicated himself to developing a quadruplex telegraph system, allowing the simultaneous transmission of four messages over a single wire. His innovative design, inspired by an insight he gained in England, bypassed the primary challenge encountered in his diplex system. The issue arose from the fact that transmitting one message could inadvertently disrupt the other. Unable to eliminate this disturbance at its source, he devised an electromechanical isolation method, effectively preventing interference. Edison referred to this solution as a "bug trap" showcasing his inventive strategy. [5]

The evidence of the use of "bug" within the solution of the "bug trap" can be found in one of the most interesting books I've ever come across, "The Papers of Thomas A. Edison" published by Johns Hopkins University Press. In this context, the notion of Bug as problems or malfunctions in the operation of a machine or device was widely known and understood. becoming commonly used in magazines and publications of that time.

One notable reference supporting this claim is the Journal titled "The Operator" The telegraph operators' journal. It serves as a practical guide to the use of the new technologies of time, such as the telegraph and the telephone. In "The Operator", the term "bug" is used to refer to the technical problems and malfunctions of various inventions. And curiously in this journal Edison and his inventions of the time were mentioned.

In the March 1, 1875, edition of "The Operator" journal, Volume III. [6], Interestingly, in this edition, we can already observe the use of the term "bug." (It is worth noting that this publication predates Edison's 1876 notes and the letters to Theodore Puskas, the president of Western Union)

Let's analyze the usage of the term in this magazine:

- On page 10 in the "Domestic Notes" session you can read it.

The Boston Quadruplex with Gerritt Smith's new double decked relays does not have a solitary " bug" upon it.

This short sentence highlights the outstanding performance of the Boston Quadruplex with Gerritt Smith's new double-decked relays. It emphasizes that no issues or failures, known as "bugs," have been found in its operation.

- Then on page 5, in the article titled "The Lively Annunciator - The lake trip."

The passage describes the discovery of a significant issue, referred to as a "bug," in the U.S. Hotel Electric Annunciator. The annunciator is described as the largest ever made and an impressive piece of equipment. However, it has recently encountered problems that have frustrated the electrician responsible for its maintenance.

The excerpt highlights the complexity of the annunciator, with around five hundred circuits and approximately thirty-six miles of wire concealed within the plastering. Despite the efforts of the linemen working for the Western Union, they have been unable to locate the source of the problem or "trouble." This situation has led to frustration and dissatisfaction, as indicated by the mention of profanity and woe-filled emotions expressed by the electrician.

In summary, the passage discusses the discovery of a major issue or malfunction, referred to as a "bug," in the U.S. Hotel Electric Annunciator. The complexity of the equipment and the difficulties in identifying and resolving the problem are emphasized.

•   At the end of the article "The new office. - The forces and its aspiration Chief Chase after a Bug" on page 8.

It recounts the story of an incident that occurred in Saratoga, and how the operators tried to fix a bug in a quad machine. The story revolves around two operators, one of whom claimed to know "everything about quads". And another operator, Ned, humbler, who generously praised others but never took credit for himself. The bottom line is that Ned managed to fix a bug that was caused by the "expert artist" who knew it all.

In the text, it can be read:

"The bug was caused by the aforesaid 'artist' attempting to balance in the small box rheostat."

The widespread use of the term "Bugs" in the technological slang of the time indicates that it was a well-established term within the community of inventors and engineers. It served as a convenient shorthand to describe the challenges and obstacles encountered during the development and refinement of technological innovations. In the course of my research, I did not find any additional prior evidence to what was mentioned earlier. Nevertheless, it is evident that this term gained notable popularity during that time due to its association with Edison's groundbreaking inventions.

Use of the term "Bug" in the late 19th and early 20th centuries.

After Edison's uses of bug in the late 1800s and early 1900s, we can find this term appearing in several related contexts, always referring to a malfunction. The Standard Electrical Dictionary was published by T. O'Conor Sloane in 1892. This book includes a definition of the term bug, describing it as

"any fault or trouble in the connections or working of electric apparatus." [7]

The January 1924 issue of The Monitor (a magazine published by Mountain States Telephone and Telegraph Company in Denver, Colorado) [8] refers to the term bug. The article titled "Repairmen" on page 14 discusses the work being done by telephone repairmen in some areas of Denver, mentioning that one of them (F. S. Philo) had 22 years of experience repairing telephones and that they expected him to continue "shoot[ing] bugs" for another 22 years. This phrase, found in the following excerpt, refers to the work of telephone repairmen in finding and fixing malfunctions in telephones.

F.S. Philo has 36 years, 22 of which have been spent repairing telephones, and, to put it in his own words, he has walked 70,000 miles, or nearly three times around the world, in the 22 years he has been a repairman. Mr. Philo may be old in service, but he is the youngest "old man" one ever met. And I hope he will continue to "shoot bugs" for another 22 years.

In the same issue of The Monitor, the comic strip "Hattie the Hello Girl" by Cy Meyn humorously uses the term bug hunter in its punchline. At the time, the term was commonly confused with its literal meaning. In this comic, Hattie buys a "Chinese back scratcher" from a bug hunter.

Image 1. Comic strip "Hattie the Hello Girl" by Cy Meyn

Hattie: *I heard you are a bug-hunter with the telephone co. So I bought you a Chinese back scratcher.*

Repair-Man: *Migosh, Hattie – Don't you know that a "bug hunter" is just a nickname for repair-man?*

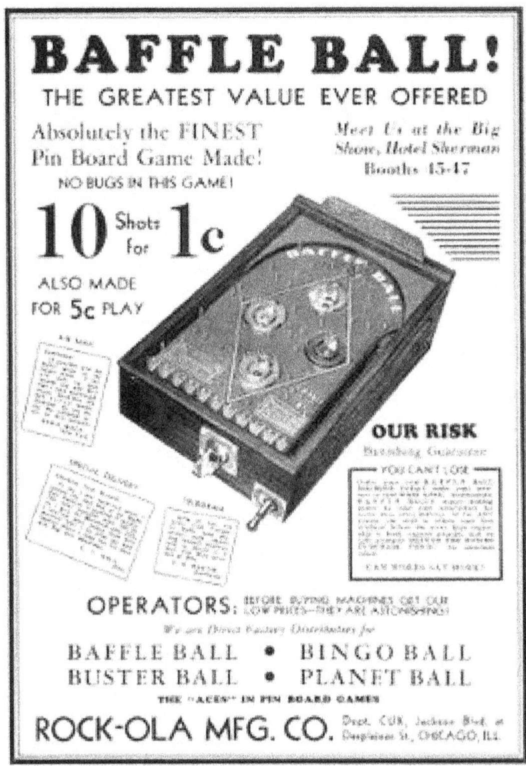

Image 2. The first mechanical pinball game "Baffle Ball"

The first mechanical pinball game, Baffle Ball, was manufactured by David Gottlieb & Company in 1931.[9] One of its advertising images, includes a sentence that reads:

"No bug in this game!" showing how common the term had become in the early 1900s.

During World War II, problems with military equipment were also called bugs. A Life magazine article from June 29th, 1942, titled "Modern Aircraft Carriers are Result of 20 Years of Smart Experimentation," [10] mentions that some errors found in the airplanes have been corrected:

"Some bugs which showed up in her design were corrected for the Yorktown and Enterprise, commissioned in 1937 and 1938..."

The term has gained such widespread popularity that it is also observable in various literary works. Two instances illustrating this phenomenon can be found in the following books, where the term 'bug' is employed within the context of system malfunction.

Louise Dickinson Rich's 1942 book We Took to the Woods includes a relevant passage about a motorized ice cutting machine:

"Ice sawing was suspended until the manufacturer could be brought in to get the bugs out of his darling..."

Famed science fiction author Isaac Asimov's 1944 story "Catch That Rabbit" uses the term bug to refer to a problem with a robot:

"U.S. Robots had to get the bugs out of the multiple robots, and there were plenty of bugs, and there are always at least half a dozen bugs left for the field testing." [11]

First actual case of a bug being found.

The first actual case of a bug being found is a historic event in the world of computing. The incident happened in the summer of 1945 at Harvard University's Mark II Aiken Relay Calculator. The Mark II was one of the first electromechanical computers ever built, and it was used by the U.S. Navy for calculations related to World War II. [12]

The Mark II was a massive machine that stood over 50 feet long and weighed more than 20 tons. It was made up of more than 750,000 individual components, including thousands of relays and switches. It was designed to perform complex calculations quickly and accurately, and it was considered one of the most advanced computing machines of its time.

However, like all complex machines, the Mark II was not without its problems. In the summer of 1945, operators of the Mark II began to notice that the machine was producing inaccurate results. The errors were sporadic and unpredictable, and they were causing serious problems for the Navy's calculations.

The operators of the Mark II began a painstaking process of trying to identify the source of the errors. They checked and double-checked the machine's relays and switches, looking for any signs of wear or damage. They also examined the programming of the machine, trying to identify any errors in the code that might be causing the problem.

After several days of investigation, the operators of the Mark II finally discovered the source of the problem. It turned out that a small moth had become trapped in one of the machine's relays, the trapped insect had caused the machine to experience operation problems. The engineers involved put the insect in one of the logbooks and called it the "first actual case of bug found." [13]

Among the team who found the first-reported computer bug was computer-language pioneer Grace Hopper. Many people believe that it was her who found the bug and who called it the "first actual case of a bug found." But there are other historical references that disprove this assertion. For example, according to the Smithsonian's National Museum of American History website,

"This logbook was probably not Hopper's, but she and the rest of the Mark II team helped popularize the use of the term computer bug and the related phrase debug."

Likewise, Peter Wayner's article "Smithsonian Honors the Original Bug in the System" includes the following passage:[14]

Peggy Kidwell, the curator who designed the exhibit, is setting the record straight. "There is a widely propagated myth that this is the first use of the term computer bug and Grace Hopper was the one who discovered it," she said. "Neither of those myths, although they are both very appealing, are true." She points out that the note in the logbook was not made in Hopper's handwriting.

This confusion may have arisen because of Grace Hopper's reputation as a pioneer in computer science who was a very knowledgeable and enthusiastic computer engineer throughout her life. She was the author of several programming books that included the word bug in their glossaries. The museum curator even mentions that Grace Hopper created a series of humorous illustrations of the different types of computer bugs infesting the Mark II computer. There is no doubt that the moth incident contributed to the widespread use and acceptance of the term within the computer sciences field, and it was Hopper who likely made the incident famous, even if she may not have originally coined the term.

Chapter 2:

FUNCTIONAL ERROR STORIES

28

Electronic Numerical Integrator and Computer.

The Electronic Numerical Integrator and Computer (ENIAC) was one of the first electronic computers built during World War II to help with military calculations. It was an impressive machine, weighing over 27 tons and consisting of more than 17,000 vacuum tubes, 70,000 resistors, and 10,000 capacitors.

The ENIAC was a massive leap forward in computing technology, but like all new technologies, it had its share of problems. It used a unique system of interconnecting cables and switches to program the computer, which meant that programming errors could be challenging to identify and fix.

The team was constantly working to improve the computer's programming, but they still encountered errors on a regular basis. During the development and early use of this computer, one of the most significant problems was the frequent failure of vacuum tubes. Vacuum tubes were used to amplify and switch electrical signals, and they were a crucial component of the computer's circuitry.

Unfortunately, the vacuum tubes used were not very reliable, and they had a relatively short lifespan. Almost every day, several tubes would burn out, which would cause the ENIAC to malfunction and be unable to perform its calculations. This meant that the computer was not operational for a significant portion of the time, which was a significant problem for the scientists and engineers who relied on the computer for their work. One of the reasons for the frequent tube failures was the high operating temperature. The computer generated a significant amount of heat, which caused the vacuum tubes to overheat and fail. In addition, the vibration and shock caused by the operation of the computer also contributed to tube failures.

To address this problem, the team tried to develop better vacuum tubes that were more reliable and could withstand the high temperatures and shock of the computer's operation. However, it was not until 1948 that special high-reliability tubes were developed that could meet the requirements.

This may not seem like a big deal today, but at the time, it was a groundbreaking discovery. It was one of the first computers to use electronic components, and the idea that a hardware problem could cause a software failure was a new concept. The discovery of the failure was a significant milestone in the history of computing, and it led to the development of new testing and debugging techniques that are still used today. [15]

The Morris Internet worm.

Robert Morris is popularly known as the creator of the Morris Worm. In 1988, this Cornell University student created a computer "worm" as part of an experiment that ended up crashing tens of thousands of computers due to a coding error. The worm – a term referring to malware that spreads through computer networks – was initially created by Morris as an experiment to measure the size of ARPANET, an experimental computer network that was the forerunner of the Internet.

The worm spread widely because it had multiple attack vectors, exploiting a backdoor in the Internet e-mail system and a bug in the "finger" program that identified network users. It was also designed to remain hidden.

The worm did not damage or destroy files, but it was still very powerful. Many services at universities and other organizations slowed down during this critical situation, with emails delayed for weeks. Many organizations began to take desperate actions such as deleting their files, while others disconnected their computers from the network for a week.

A bug in the code transformed the worm from a potentially harmless and intellectual computing exercise into a viral denial of service attack. The worm started replicating itself on each computer several times, slowing these computers down to the point of rendering them unusable.

Morris was convicted of violating the Computer Fraud and Abuse Act of 1986, resulting in a three-year prison sentence, 400 hours of community service, and a $10,000 fine.

A Harvard spokesman estimated the economic damages at between $100,000 and $10,000,000. Currently, the Morris worm source code is kept on a 3.5 floppy disk at The Computer History Museum. A text accompanying the disk reads:

This disk contains the complete source code of the Morris Internet worm program. This tiny, 99-line program brought large pieces of the Internet to a standstill on November 2nd, 1988. The worm was the first of many intrusive programs that use the Internet to spread.

One of the positive aspects of such events is that, since this incident, network security issues have become a major concern. [16][17]

Hartford Civic Center coliseum collapse.

A New York Times article from January 19, 1978, reports on the collapse of a Connecticut civic center the previous day:

Under a heavy blanket of ice and snow, the huge flat roof of the two-year-old Hartford Civic Center's coliseum collapsed at 4:15 this morning, raining havoc on the $70 million convention and shopping complex that was meant to be the centerpiece of the city's resurgence.

Fortunately, no one was in the building, and no one was injured. Even though the roof had been designed and tested with a complex computer program, the unique structure consisted of unusual pyramidal trusses and was supported by only four columns so that spectators would have an unobstructed view. The roof was notable for being one of the first large-scale roofs made possible by computer design and analysis.

There are many opinions about possible causes of the collapse, one of which believes that the programmer of the CAD software used to design the coliseum incorrectly assumed the steel roof support would only face pure compression. In addition, the computer model assumed that all the top chords were laterally braced, while, in reality, only the interior structure met the criteria. The total cost of the mistake was over $70 million, plus another $20 million for damage to the local economy. The roof was rebuilt in 1980 – bigger and better – and is still unbent on the same four columns over what is now the XL Center. These columns are 12 feet taller, allowing for more seating. [18][19]

Kerberos random number generator.

Kerberos is a protocol created by the Massachusetts Institute of Technology used to authenticate two devices that connect to each other. This does not mean, however, that it will authorize them; it just authenticates them. Its function is to identify each user by encryption.

Some of the requirements of the protocol are that: authentication must be bi-directional, no clear-text passwords are transmitted over the network, no clear-text passwords are stored on servers, clients must use clear-text passwords for as short a time as possible, the authentication must have a limited lifetime, and it must be transparent to the user.

The basic "currency" of the Kerberos authentication protocol is a credential or capability known as a ticket. The possession of a ticket and its accompanying session key determines the ability to use a service. Kerberos makes use of random session keys for authenticating transactions.

Knowledge of these secret keys is used as proof of identity and for verifying the authenticity of messages. If one of the keys is compromised, then anything authenticated by that key cannot be trusted.

When a bug was discovered in the random number generator of the Netscape web browser, it caused Kerberos to take a closer look at its own random number generator. The flaw in Netscape would allow network users to intercept and decrypt potentially sensitive information such as credit card numbers. Jeffrey I. Schiller, Manager of Network Systems and Operations and one of the developers of Kerberos, said that the Kerberos random number generator was predictable: "If you knew when someone logged on, you could figure out the session key."

After examining the Kerberos code, the Institute's researchers discovered a flaw with the random number generator. The problem was solved by inserting the correct random number generator code into the flawed version. Steve Lodin and Bryn Dole, two graduate students at Purdue, discovered that the flaw would allow unauthorized users to gain access to the Kerberos' secret "tickets" in less than five minutes. There was arguably a vulnerability that had been present for several years and was caused by an error in the code, but there is no evidence that it was used by people during the time it was there. Again, the error's potential for damages is the most interesting and crucial takeaway. [20][21]

AT&T network failure.

American Telephone & Telegraph (AT&T) is an American multinational corporation headquartered in Dallas, Texas; it is one of the largest telecommunications companies in the world. In January of 1990, a bug in a new version of the software that controlled AT&T's #4ESS long distance switches caused these computers to crash when they received a specific message from other related machines.

According to Larry Seese, AT&T's Director of Technology Development, the "fault was in the code" of the new software that AT&T loaded into front-end processors. The New York switch informed its connected 4ESS switches that it couldn't handle more calls. Seese called this message a 'congestion signal.' Once the switch finished restarting, New York's switch became operational again and started handling calls. This is when the problem with the new software became evident.

Technicians had upgraded the software to accelerate the processing of certain types of messages. Although the code was tested, a one-line bug was added to the recovery software of each of the switches in the network. The defect was in a C program that featured a break statement located within an if clause, that was nested within a switch clause.

This failure of AT&T's systems caused sixty thousand people to completely lose their phone service. During the nine long hours of hard work by technicians trying to restore service, some seventy million phone calls were dropped. [22][23]

Incorrect divisions on Intel Pentium processors.

If you still have a computer with a Pentium processor at 60, 66, 75, 90, or 100 MHz, you can reproduce this popular error. Let's start by completing the following calculation: the first number is 4195835.0 divided by the second number 3145727.0. The correct value should be 1.333 820 449 136 241 000. If you use a computer with the above-mentioned characteristics, however, the value for the same calculation would be 1.333 739 068 902 037 589, which is incorrect.

This bug, also popularly known as the Pentium FDIV bug, was a hardware bug affecting the floating-point unit (FPU) of early Intel Pentium processors. Due to this bug, the processor would return incorrect binary floating-point results when dividing certain pairs of high-precision numbers. It was discovered in 1994 by Thomas Nicely, a professor of mathematics at Lynchburg College, when he realized that some division operations always returned an erroneous excess value. Other people quickly confirmed the same errors in the divisions.

Intel refused to replace all defective microprocessors; however, if a person could prove that they had been affected by the bug, then Intel would proceed to replace their processor. With an estimated three to five million defective chips in circulation, eventually the company relented and agreed to replace chips for anyone who complained. The failure ended up costing Intel $475 million, once again showing the large-scale effects of small-scale errors. [24][25][26]

The Y2K Bug.

On December 31, 1999, humanity was preparing to welcome not just a new year, but also a new century and millennium. Amidst many apocalyptic and catastrophic predictions, the world witnessed widespread concern about the Y2K bug, also known as "2000" which was a computer error caused by the habit of omitting the century (e.g., "19") when programming the date, assuming that the software would only be in operation between 1900 and 1999.

Some years earlier, however, some atypical behaviors related to dates were already being detected in some computers. Such is the case when a batch of corned beef was rejected by a supermarket because it appeared to be more than 80 years old or when, in 1993, Mary Bandar, a 104-year-old woman from Minnesota was invited to start kindergarten because, according to the computer records, she was just four years old. State computers mistook her as a four-year-old because "89" was the only input for her birthdate.

This problem has arisen since 1951, when the first commercial computers appeared in Great Britain through the company J. Lyons and Co. In order to save space and speed up processing, dates were abbreviated in computer data by omitting the century (e.g., January 1, 1900, was 01/01/00 and December 31, 1999, was 12/31/99). For dates within the same century, no errors would be generated, but they would be for dates in different centuries, as in the case of Mary Bandar, America's oldest kindergartener.

This growing concern about Y2K was so worrying that even President Clinton announced a campaign in mid-1998 to share information and solutions to the potential coming crisis. On this topic, Clinton said:

No one will ever find every embedded microchip, every line of code that needs to be rewritten. But if companies, agencies and organizations are ready, if they understand the threat and have backup plans, then we will meet this challenge.

Clinton also pledged to help other countries combat the Y2K crisis by providing $12 million to raise awareness of the error in developing countries. The Y2K crisis didn't happen on a large scale because people started preparing for it more than a decade in advance, and, while some people consider the whole thing to have been a hoax or a myth, there were a lot of reported system failures.

The age of a baby born in Denmark just after the start of the new millennium was recorded as 100 years. Some U.S. spy satellites were disrupted for three days due to a temporary and problematic fix required for this bug. In South Korea, thermostat failures were recorded, and, in Australia, bus ticket machines broke down. In the United States, lottery machines failed in Delaware. These are all signs that we should remain alert and prepared, because a similar problem is expected to occur by 2038 for computers running 32-bit operating systems. [27][28][29]

Gangnam Style video broke YouTube's view counters.

"Gangnam Style, the 2012 hit song by Korean hip-hop star Psy, quickly became the most viewed YouTube video of all time. Many of us witnessed Psy's horse dance move immortalized by the song's accompanying music video. We also witnessed the YouTube view counter growing rapidly over the weeks until it was the platform's most viewed video. When the site's view counter for Gangnam Style reached 2,147,483,647 views, it started to show the views as negative numbers – surely frustrating for Psy's fans.

The reason behind this was that YouTube's counter previously used a 32-bit integer, which is a unit used to represent data in computer architecture. This means that the maximum possible views it could count was 2,147,483,647.

When the programmers built YouTube, they probably never imagined a video garnering so many views, so the code didn't take higher numbers into account. Google, the then-owner of YouTube, made a statement about the incident, explaining "We never thought a video would be watched in numbers greater than a 32-bit integer... but that was before we met Psy."

The solution from YouTube was to begin using a 64-bit integer video counter, which means videos now have a maximum view count of 9.22 quintillion – 9,223,372,036,854,775,808 to be exact. Now the South Korean singer can rest easy, as he (probably) won't need another update and adjustment from YouTube in the future. If you don't think that number is high enough, I invite you to try saying it out loud in less than 10 seconds: nine quintillion, two hundred and twenty-three quadrillion, three hundred and seventy-two trillion, thirty-six billion, eight hundred and fifty-four million, seven hundred and seventy-five thousand, eight hundred and eight. [30][31]

The north-east US power outage

On August 14, 2003, the Northeastern United States and parts of Canada were plunged into darkness during the largest power outage in North American history. The blackout affected an estimated 50 million people across eight US states and parts of Canada. The cause of the outage was ultimately determined to be a software bug in the alarm system of a power company control room.

The incident began at 2:14 p.m., when a power plant in Ohio tripped offline due to a voltage sag. This led to a chain reaction of power plant shutdowns, in turn causing a domino effect of power losses throughout the Northeastern region. The outage lasted for several days in some areas, resulting in widespread disruptions in transportation, communication, and commerce.

The root cause of the outage was traced back to a software bug in the alarm system of FirstEnergy, the power company responsible for the plant in Ohio that initially went offline. The alarm system was designed to alert operators of problems within the power grid, such as power fluctuations or equipment failures. However, the system was configured to only trigger alarms if more than three sensors detected a problem within a specified time frame. This configuration had been put in place to reduce the number of false alarms that operators had to deal with on a daily basis.

On the day of the outage, the voltage sag caused by the power plant shutdown triggered only two sensors. As a result, the alarm system did not alert the control room, and the control room operators were unaware of the problem. By the time the operators realized what was happening, it was too late to prevent the cascade of power plant shutdowns that led to the blackout.

The software bug that caused the alarm system to fail was a simple coding error. The system was designed to use a logical AND operator instead of a logical OR operator when determining if an alarm should be triggered. This meant that, if any of the sensors failed to detect a problem, the entire alarm system would fail to trigger an alert.

This incident highlights the importance of software quality assurance and testing in critical infrastructure systems. It also led to changes in the way that power companies monitor and manage the electrical grid to prevent similar incidents from occurring in the future. Additionally, the incident led to increased attention and investment in the development of smart grid technologies, which use advanced sensors and software to monitor and manage the power grid in real-time. [32] [33]

British Passports to Nowhere.

In 1999, the British government introduced a new passport processing system called the Computerisation of the Passport and Nationality Services (COTS) program. The new system was intended to streamline the passport application process and improve security features.

However, shortly after the system was launched, problems began to arise. A software bug caused passport applications to be lost or delayed, and, in some cases, passports were issued with incorrect information or to the wrong person. These problems caused significant delays and frustration for travelers, with some people waiting for weeks or even months for their passports to be issued. The situation was exacerbated by the fact that many people were applying for passports in advance of upcoming millennium celebrations, which led to a surge in demand.

The software bug was eventually traced to an issue with the way that the COTS system was handling data. The system used a new database to store passport application information, but a bug in the system meant that data was being lost or overwritten during the processing of applications.

The British government initially attempted to downplay the severity of the issue, but, as the number of delayed passports continued to grow, it became clear that the problem was more widespread than initially thought. The government was criticized for its handling of the situation, with many people expressing frustration at the lack of information and the slow response from officials. The Home Office, which was responsible for the passport processing system, was forced to issue an apology and promised to take action to resolve the issue. With the help of outside contractors, the government was able to fix the problems with the passport system. The cost of fixing the issue and dealing with the backlog of delayed passport applications was estimated to be in the millions of pounds.

In the aftermath of the incident, the government launched an inquiry into what had gone wrong with the COTS system. The inquiry identified a range of issues, including a lack of proper testing and inadequate training for staff. The report made a series of recommendations for improving the system and preventing similar incidents from happening in the future.

The British Passports to Nowhere incident was a significant embarrassment for the government, and it highlighted the potential risks of implementing new systems without thoroughly testing them first. It also serves as a reminder of the importance of proper data management and the need to have contingency plans in place in the event of system failures. [34][35]

Windows 98 crashed live.

On June 10, 1998, Microsoft founder Bill Gates gave a live demonstration of the new Windows 98 operating system at the COMDEX computer trade show in Las Vegas. However, things didn't go as planned, with the system crashing in front of the audience and Gates scrambling to regain control.

The demonstration was intended to showcase the new features and capabilities of Windows 98, which was set to be released later that month. Gates began by showing off the new Plug and Play feature that was supposed to make it easy to connect and use new devices with the computer. However, when he tried to plug in a scanner to demonstrate the feature, the system froze and displayed an error message. Gates attempted to troubleshoot the issue, but the error persisted, causing the system to crash completely. As the audience looked on, Gates attempted to restart the system, but the error message continued to appear, prompting him to joke, "It must be Windows

98."

The incident quickly became a viral sensation, with media outlets around the world reporting on the embarrassing moment for the tech giant. Critics of Microsoft pointed to the incident as evidence of the company's lack of reliability and quality control, while others noted the irony of the crash given the company's slogan at the time: Where do you want to go today?

Despite the setback, Windows 98 was ultimately released as scheduled later that month, and it went on to become one of Microsoft's most successful operating systems, with an estimated 25 million copies sold in its first year on the market.

The incident also served as a wake-up call for the tech industry as a whole, highlighting the need for more rigorous testing and quality control processes to prevent similar embarrassments in the future. Since then, tech companies have invested heavily in testing and quality assurance measures, with many now employing dedicated teams of testers and engineers to ensure that their products are reliable and user-friendly.

In the end, the Windows 98 crash live on stage with Bill Gates was a moment that captured the public's attention and helped to usher in a new era of scrutiny and accountability for the tech industry. Despite the initial embarrassment, Microsoft was ultimately able to recover and continue its dominance in the computer market while also learning valuable lessons about the importance of quality control and testing in new technology development. [36][37]

Reebok's free trainers.

In 2012, Reebok ran a promotion in the United States, offering free custom-designed sneakers to customers who used the company's YourReebok website to create their own unique design. However, due to a software bug in the ordering system, the sneakers were being offered for free to anyone who used a certain promo code, regardless of whether they had actually designed the sneakers on the website or not.

As word of the promotion spread online, the promo code quickly went viral, and thousands of people took advantage of the glitch in the system to order free sneakers. In some cases, customers placed orders for dozens or even hundreds of pairs of shoes, costing Reebok enormous sums of money. The total cost of the promotion quickly spiraled out of control, with estimates ranging from tens of thousands to millions of dollars in losses. Some reports suggest that the company was on the hook for more than $5 million in fraudulent orders before the promotion was finally shut down.

Reebok was forced to issue a public statement acknowledging the error and apologizing to customers who had legitimately used the YourReebok website to create custom sneakers. The company also promised to investigate the issue and take steps to prevent similar glitches from occurring in the future.

While the incident was certainly embarrassing for Reebok, it also highlights the potential risks associated with software bugs in e-commerce systems. A seemingly minor glitch in the code can quickly lead to enormous losses if left unchecked, especially when large-scale promotions or other marketing efforts are involved.

In the wake of the incident, Reebok likely took steps to improve its testing and quality assurance procedures to ensure that similar bugs are caught and addressed before they have the chance to cause serious damage to the company's bottom line or reputation. Additionally, the incident serves as a reminder to other companies to be vigilant when it comes to e-commerce systems, especially large-scale marketing efforts that could be vulnerable to exploitation by savvy customers or hackers. [38][39][40]

Internal Revenue Service.

The IRS e-file system is utilized by millions of Americans annually for electronically submitting their tax returns, offering a faster and more efficient alternative to the traditional paper filing method. Tax professionals also rely on the e-file system to submit returns on behalf of their clients. However, over the years, this system has encountered a series of challenges, including errors that have caused frustration for both taxpayers and tax preparers.

Some of these errors have included:

- Technical Issues with Online Payment Portal: The IRS faced technical difficulties with its online payment portal, impacting taxpayers attempting to make tax payments online on the last day of the tax filing deadline. These issues arose from errors in the payment processing system, prompting the IRS to extend the deadline for affected individuals.

- Errors in the Withholding Calculator: In response to changes in tax law, the IRS introduced a new withholding tax calculator. Unfortunately, this calculator contained errors that resulted in some taxpayers experiencing either insufficient or excessive withholdings in their paychecks. To rectify the situation, the IRS issued an apology and recommended that taxpayers review and adjust their withholdings as needed.
- System Outage: During the 2021 tax season, the IRS encountered an outage in its electronic filing system (e-File). This outage led to difficulties for both taxpayers and tax preparers attempting to electronically file their tax returns. As a solution, the IRS extended the filing deadline for returns affected by the outage, providing additional time for taxpayers to submit their documents.

Despite these challenges, the IRS has consistently and resolutely responded to address errors in its software systems. The agency has made efforts to enhance the scalability and capacity of its systems to better accommodate the demands of the tax season. Additionally, measures have been implemented to bolster the security of taxpayers' information.

One noteworthy initiative by the IRS is its commitment to transparency regarding software errors. Since 2003, the IRS has made error reports publicly accessible. These reports comprehensively outline the nature of the errors, specify whether they have been resolved, and detail how they have impacted taxpayers and tax preparers. This transparency empowers those affected by these errors to gain a deeper understanding of the issues and explore potential solutions. [41][42][43]

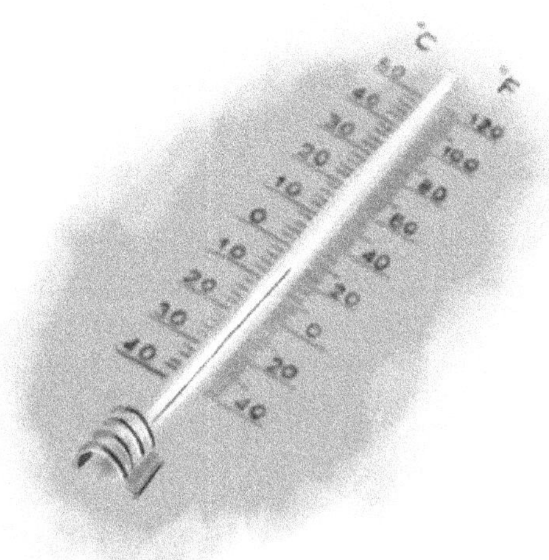

Thermostat bug Leaves People in the Cold.

The Nest Thermostat, created by Nest Labs, is a popular and innovative home automation device that allows users to remotely control their home's temperature and save energy. However, in January 2016, a software glitch left some Nest Thermostat users in the cold – literally.

The glitch affected the third-generation Nest Thermostat, causing the device's battery to drain rapidly, which in turn caused the thermostat to shut down. As a result, some users found themselves waking up to cold houses in the middle of winter with no way to turn on the heat.

Nest Labs quickly acknowledged the problem and released a software update to fix it, but the incident highlighted the potential dangers of relying too heavily on technology in our homes.

The Nest Thermostat is designed to learn the habits of its users and adjust the temperature accordingly. For example, if a user typically lowers the temperature at night, the thermostat will learn this and do it automatically. This feature is meant to save energy and make the user's life easier, but it also means that users may not be in the habit of manually adjusting the thermostat as they might have done in the past.

When the glitch occurred, some users found themselves without heat for several hours until they realized what was happening and manually turned on their heating systems. While home automation devices like the Nest Thermostat can make our lives easier and more efficient, they are not infallible, and users should always have a backup plan in case of a glitch or malfunction.

The incident also raises questions about the responsibility companies like Nest Labs have to ensure that their products are reliable and safe. While Nest Labs quickly addressed the problem and released a fix, the fact that the glitch occurred in the first place is cause for concern. As home automation devices become more prevalent, companies that create these devices will need to be more diligent in testing and ensuring the reliability of their products. [44][45]

Nasdaq "flash freeze" in 2013.

The Nasdaq Stock Market is one of the largest electronic stock exchanges in the world, handling more than two billion trades per day. It is known for its fast and efficient trading systems that allow investors to buy and sell shares quickly and easily. However, the exchange has a history of technical issues, including Facebook's botched initial public offering (IPO) in May 2012, which resulted in losses for many investors.

On August 22, 2013, Nasdaq experienced a major technical issue that would come to be known as the "flash freeze glitch." At approximately 12:14 p.m. Eastern Time, the trading of more than 3,000 stocks was halted due to a technical issue. The issue was initially believed to be a glitch in the exchange's Securities Information Processor (SIP), which is a system that disseminates stock quotes and trades to the public. As soon as the outage occurred, Nasdaq issued a statement acknowledging the problem and stating that it was investigating the cause. The statement read, in part:

Nasdaq OMX halted trading in all Tape C securities at 12:14:03 p.m. ET on Thursday, August 22, 2013, due to a technical issue with the system that consolidates and disseminates quote and trade information for Nasdaq-listed securities. We are working with other exchanges that are affected by this issue and will provide further information as soon as possible.

The outage lasted for approximately three hours, during which time investors were unable to buy or sell shares of the affected stocks. The incident had a major impact on the stock market, with some stocks experiencing significant price swings when trading resumed. Some investors were left holding shares that they had intended to sell, while others were unable to buy shares they had intended to purchase.

In the aftermath of the flash freeze glitch, Nasdaq launched an investigation into the cause of the outage. The investigation revealed that the problem was not with the SIP system, as had been initially suspected, but with a software bug in the trading system itself. The bug was related to a software update for the system implemented the previous day. The software update was intended to improve the system's ability to handle a high volume of messages. However, the update contained a flaw that caused the system to become overwhelmed when it received many orders. This led to a cascade of failures in the system, ultimately resulting in the outage.

The software bug was caused by a coding error in the trading system's software. Specifically, the software contained a race condition, which is a type of programming error that occurs when two or more processes access a shared resource in an unexpected way. In this case, the race condition occurred when the system received a large number of order cancellations, which overwhelmed and crashed the system. [46][47][48][49]

Chapter 3:

AEROSPACE ERROR STORIES

The Mariner 1 spacecraft

In July of 1962, NASA launched an unmanned space mission from Cape Canaveral, commencing the first Mariner mission. Its objective was to perform a flyby of Venus, but the journey did not go as planned. The spacecraft was destroyed by the Range Safety Officer 293 seconds after launch (09:26:16 UT) when it veered off course.

The booster had been operating satisfactorily until an unscheduled lift maneuver was detected. The faulty application of guidance commands made steering impossible, meaning that the spacecraft could possibly crash into shipping areas in the North Atlantic or inhabited areas on land if not destroyed in the air.

The incident was caused by a combination of factors, one of which related to the mistaken omission of a hyphen in coded computer instructions in the craft's data-editing program, resulting in the transmission of incorrect guidance signals to the spacecraft.

As a result of that omission, the computer processed the data incorrectly, interpreted erratic behavior where there was none, and, in trying to correct the "problem," actually caused erratic behavior. The cost of the Mariner 1 was as high as $18.5 million in 1962; adjusted to today's rates, that would be about $169 million.

There has been a great deal of speculation about the failure of Mariner 1, with some attributing it to the pressure of the space race between the United States and the Soviet Union in the 1960s. On December 14, 1962, Mariner 2 (the backup craft for the Mariner 1 mission) became the first robotic space probe to conduct a successful planetary encounter, reaching Venus and returning data on its atmosphere, magnetic field, charged particle environment, and the mass of the planet. In addition, this ambitious and million-dollar project taught us the cost of an error as minute as omitting a hyphen.

Following the Mariner 1 mishap, NASA underwent a rigorous review of its systems and processes. This event prompted a comprehensive reassessment of the software validation and verification procedures. The agency implemented stringent checks, introducing new layers of redundancy and error-detection mechanisms to prevent similar coding errors. The incident served as a pivotal moment, emphasizing the critical importance of precise programming in space exploration endeavors. NASA's response to the failure of Mariner 1 not only marked a technological evolution but also underscored the invaluable lessons learned from even the smallest oversights in mission-critical programming. [50]

ESA Ariane 5 Flight V88, 1996

The ESA (European Space Agency) Ariane 5 Flight V88 launch on June 4, 1996, was a catastrophic failure caused by a software error that destroyed the rocket less than a minute after takeoff. The rocket was launched from the Kourou spaceport in French Guiana, carrying four satellites valued at around $500 million.

The Ariane 5 rocket was designed to launch commercial payloads into space and was intended to be an upgrade to the earlier Ariane 4 rocket. The upgraded rocket was built with more powerful engines and a new guidance system designed to make the rocket more accurate and more efficient than its predecessor. The software used to control the rocket's guidance system was taken from the Ariane 4 and adapted for use in the Ariane 5.

The software issue that caused the rocket to fail was a result of a data conversion error. The guidance system on the rocket used a 64-bit floating-point number to represent the horizontal velocity of the rocket. However, the software that controlled the guidance system had been designed for the Ariane 4 rocket, which had a maximum horizontal velocity of 64 meters per second. The Ariane 5 rocket, on the other hand, had a maximum horizontal velocity of 250 meters per second.

The conversion of the 64-bit floating-point number to a 16-bit signed integer led to an overflow error that caused the guidance system to fail. The error occurred just 39 seconds after liftoff when the rocket had reached an altitude of around 4 km and was traveling at a speed of around 700 m/s. The rocket's guidance system issued an emergency shutdown command, causing the rocket's engines to cut out, and it lost control.

The rocket then broke apart and exploded, with debris scattering across the launch site. Fortunately, no one was injured in the incident, but the cost of the failure was estimated to be around $370 million, with the loss of the four valuable satellites and the costs associated with the investigation and repair of the damage caused by the explosion. [51][52][53]

Mars Climate Orbiter met a catastrophic fate.

In the poignant month of September 1999, following a nearly 10-month interstellar voyage, the Mars Climate Orbiter (MCO) met a catastrophic fate, shattering into fragments. Despite the NASA engineers' anticipation for a momentous celebration, reality dealt a different hand, all due to an oversight in employing the proper units – the metric system! The Scientific American Space Lab released an engaging video on this very subject.

Built at a staggering cost of $125 million, the Mars Climate Orbiter was a 638-kilogram robotic emissary propelled into space by NASA on December 11, 1998, with the mission to investigate the Martian climate, atmosphere, and surface metamorphosis.

The ambitious vision was to establish a near-circular Sun-synchronous orbit a mere 260 miles above the Martian surface by December 1, 1999. Beyond its celestial exploration, the MCO was designed to play a vital role as a communication bridge, ensuring the seamless relay of data between Earth and the Mars Polar Lander during its mission.

Tragedy struck when the MCO's journey took an abrupt and catastrophic turn. After completing precisely scheduled course corrections and a meticulously planned Mars orbit insertion burn, all seemed well. But fate had something else in store. As the orbiter was supposed to emerge from its Martian blind spot, ready to transmit signals, there was only silence – an agonizing silence that engulfed the control room. A relentless investigation swiftly ensued, peeling back the layers of this spaceborne enigma.

The investigation report traced the catastrophic failure's origins to an insidious software error. Lockheed Martin's ground software measured results in United States customary units, which was unwittingly misaligned with NASA's expectations of SI units, heralding a catastrophic miscommunication at a crucial juncture.

The revelation was astonishingly simple yet devastating. It was all an inconspicuous discrepancy of measurement units. Commands expressed in the imperial system – pound-seconds – were unwittingly dispatched without the vital conversion to the metric standard – Newton-seconds. The dire ramifications were now apparent. The MCO had missed its intended orbit by a staggering 90 miles, veering off course by 145 kilometers.

This ill-fated error condemned the orbiter to a perilous plunge into the Martian atmosphere, subjecting it to the unforgiving atmospheric stresses that ultimately spelled its doom. The Mars Climate Orbiter, a testament to human ingenuity and ambition, was lost, its pieces scattered across the alien surface of the Red Planet. Yet, amidst the heartache and grief, lessons were learned and resilience ignited. The scientific community rallied together, more determined than ever to ensure that the orbiter's legacy would endure. This cautionary tale etched itself into the annals of space exploration, a stark reminder of the unforgiving nature of the cosmos and the significance of meticulous precision. The quest to understand Mars persisted, with each failure strengthening the resolve to seek answers beyond the reaches of our own blue planet. [54][55][56]

Failures During the Starliner's First Orbital Flight Test.

The Boeing CST-100 Starliner is a crewed spacecraft developed by Boeing for NASA's Commercial Crew Program. Its primary purpose is to transport astronauts to the International Space Station (ISS) and other low Earth orbits. The CST-100 Starliner is part of NASA's efforts to reduce dependence on Russian spacecraft and provide U.S. space agencies with greater independence in accessing space. The CST-100 Starliner has the capacity to carry up to seven astronauts and is launched using United Launch Alliance's Atlas V rockets. The spacecraft is designed to be reusable for multiple missions, making it a crucial component of NASA's space access strategy and space exploration in general.

The Boeing Starliner Orbital Flight Test marked the CST-100 Starliner's maiden voyage into space, the intention was to conduct an eight-day test to assess the spacecraft's performance, which included approaching and docking with the International Space Station (ISS) and ultimately landing in the western United States.

However, just 31 minutes after liftoff, a clock-related issue surfaced. Intermittent communication problems between the spacecraft and ground control prevented flight controllers from addressing the problem. This anomaly triggered the spacecraft's Orbital Maneuvering Thrusters (OMT) to fire in the wrong orbit, resulting in excessive propellant consumption. Consequently, the spacecraft was unable to approach and dock with the International Space Station (ISS).

It was also revealed that a second critical software error occurred during the flight, potentially leading to a collision between the service module and the Starliner after their separation. This issue was rectified just two hours before the capsule re-entered the Earth's atmosphere. Without the discovery and correction of this error, it could have jeopardized the Starliner and hindered a safe landing. Furthermore, it was determined that if the first anomaly had not occurred, the second would have gone unnoticed.

Both errors could have been caught before launch if Boeing had performed more thorough software testing on the ground, according to John Mulholland, vice president and manager of Boeing's CST-100 Starliner program. He also mentioned that the team detected that software error before Starliner began its descent procedure. The team very quickly recoded the software, reverified it in the labs, and we were able to upload that software correction and safely complete the mission.[57][58]

Software Mishap Triggers Major FAA Computer System Breakdown.

The On January 2023, a ground stop and system failures at the Federal Aviation Administration (FAA) impacted thousands of flights across the United States. According to a senior official briefed on the internal review, it appears that this was the result of an error during routine scheduled systems maintenance.

The error occurred when an engineer replaced one code file with another without realizing the mistake. As the systems began to exhibit problems and ultimately failed, FAA staff worked feverishly to determine what had gone wrong. The engineer responsible for the error was unaware of the mistake. This incident was characterized as an "honest mistake that cost the country millions." The issue led to a nationwide pause on all domestic departures until 9 a.m. The system responsible for sending flight hazards and real-time restrictions to pilots, known as the NOTAM system, experienced an outage, prompting the FAA to instruct airlines to halt all domestic departures to validate flight and safety information integrity.

The incident exposed the need to replace the outdated FAA NOTAM system, and an investigation is ongoing to determine the exact cause of the failure, there is no evidence of a cyberattack, and all possibilities are being considered to ensure FAA systems were not breached.

Transportation Secretary Pete Buttigieg emphasized the importance of a thorough investigation and possible reforms within the FAA. President Joe Biden was also briefed on the situation, and there was no evidence of a cyberattack at that time. Other politician US like Republican Sen. Ted Cruz criticized the FAA's management of the system and called for an explanation of issues.

Several airlines were impacted by delays due to these technical issues, and some allowed passengers to rebook their flights at no additional cost. [59][60]

American Airlines - Sabre System.

In 2018, American Airlines experienced a significant issue with its flight booking system that caused thousands of flights to be canceled or delayed. The issue was related to Sabre, a computer reservation system that is widely used in the travel industry.

Sabre is used by many airlines to manage flight bookings, seat assignments, and other travel-related tasks. On April 16, 2018, American Airlines noticed an issue with its Sabre system, which prevented the airline from accessing passenger reservations. This issue impacted American Airlines flights all over the world, causing significant delays and cancellations.

The issue was caused by a problem with the communication between Sabre's system and American Airlines' system. Specifically, the Sabre system was not properly syncing with American Airlines' system, which prevented the airline from accessing the passenger reservations it needed to manage its flights.

As a result of the issue, American Airlines was forced to cancel more than 2,000 flights over the course of several days. This had a significant impact on the airline's reputation and on the travel plans of thousands of passengers.

The issue with Sabre also impacted other airlines that use the system. For example, Delta Air Lines experienced a similar issue in September 2018, which caused widespread delays and cancellations.

Sabre issued a statement acknowledging the issue and apologizing for the impact it had on its customers. The company said that it was working to resolve the issue as quickly as possible and that it would continue to work with its customers to minimize the impact of the issue.

In the aftermath of the issue, American Airlines and other airlines that use Sabre called for better communication and coordination between the airlines and the reservation system providers. They also called for improved backup and redundancy measures to ensure that such issues do not occur in the future.

Overall, the American Airlines-Sabre system issue serves as a reminder of the critical role that software systems play in the travel industry. Even a small glitch or error can have a significant impact on travel plans and cause widespread disruption. It also highlights the need for robust backup and redundancy measures to ensure that critical systems can continue to operate even in the face of unexpected issues or outages. [61][62]

Heathrow Terminal 5 Opening, 2008.

The opening of Terminal 5 at London's Heathrow Airport in March 2008 was a highly anticipated event, representing a significant investment and a major expansion of the airport's capacity. However, the opening was marred by a series of technical issues, including a software glitch that caused significant disruptions to flights and left thousands of passengers stranded.

The software issue in question was related to Terminal 5's new, highly automated baggage handling system that was designed to handle up to 12,000 bags per hour. However, on the day of the opening, the system encountered a critical bug that caused it to fail, resulting in lost bags, delayed flights, and frustrated passengers. The exact cause of the bug was not immediately clear, but it was believed to be related to a conflict between the software that controlled the automated baggage system and the scanners that were used to identify and sort bags. As a result of the bug, bags were misdirected, loaded onto the wrong flights, or simply lost altogether, causing significant delays and disruptions to the airport's operations.

In the aftermath of the incident, the airport's management and the software vendor responsible for the baggage handling system – BAA and IBM, respectively – faced intense criticism from the media, passengers, and industry analysts. Many blamed the incident on poor planning, insufficient testing, and a failure to adequately prepare for the high volumes of traffic and baggage the new terminal was expected to handle.

To address the issues, BAA and IBM launched an extensive investigation into the root cause of the problem and implemented a number of corrective measures to prevent similar incidents from occurring in the future. These included improved testing and quality assurance processes, increased capabilities for dealing with redundancy and failover in the baggage handling system, and improved communication and contingency planning in the event of future disruptions.

Despite these early setbacks, Terminal 5 eventually became one of the most efficient and successful terminals at Heathrow, handling millions of passengers and bags each year with relatively few incidents. The software glitch and the ensuing chaos served as a cautionary tale about the risks and complexities of large-scale software systems and highlighted the need for thorough testing and contingency planning to mitigate those risks. [63][64]

Chapter 4:

MILITARY MISHAPS ERROR STORIES

The Soviet Oko system almost started a nuclear war.

The Cold War was a period of geopolitical tension between the United States and the Soviet Union and their respective allies. The first phase of the Cold War began after the end of World War II in 1945. By the 1980s, another period of heightened tension arose, leading the United States to increase diplomatic, military, and economic pressures against the Soviet Union. During this time, an error in the Soviet Union Oko system almost triggered a nuclear war between the two military superpowers.

Oko is a Russian (formerly Soviet) missile defense early warning program consisting of orbiting satellites. On September 26, 1983, this radar mistakenly reported the launch of intercontinental ballistic missiles from the United States. One of the officers of the Soviet Air Defense Forces, Stanislav Petrov, considered the report to be a computer error since a nuclear first strike by the United States would probably involve hundreds of simultaneous missiles launches. Petrov's suspicion was confirmed when, in fact, no missiles ever arrived. Another factor, he said, was that Soviet ground-based radar installations – which look for missiles rising over the horizon – showed no evidence of an attack.

According to the Washington Post article "I Had A Funny Feeling in My Gut" by David Hoffman, Petrov had been assigned to the satellite early warning system since its inception in the 1970s; thus, he knew firsthand that the system was flawed. It had been rushed into service, he explained in an interview, and was "raw." After this incident, he was investigated for not having followed protocol and for acting in an undisciplined manner by skipping the chain of command.

Despite the fact that Petrov gave several interviews for newspapers, magazines, and films as well as receiving awards and commendations, there is also some confusion among many critics and specialists about Petrov's "military role" in this incident. They think that Petrov, as an individual, was not in a position where he could have launched any Soviet missiles on his own. Regardless of who made the decision, what is certain is the impact an error can have on an anti-missile system. [65][66]

Failure of Patriot missile defense during the Gulf War.

The Gulf War was a war fought by a United Nations-sanctioned coalition force of 34 countries, led by the United States, against the Iraqi Republic in response to Iraq's invasion and annexation of the State of Kuwait. In this conflict, Iraq began using Scud missiles to bomb targets in Israel. In this situation, the United States had in its power to use several "anti-missile" Patriot batteries.

One of these Patriot missiles located in Dharan (Saudi Arabia) failed to track and intercept an incoming Iraqi Scud missile. A report of the General Accounting office, GAO/IMTEC-92-26, entitled Patriot Missile Defense: Software Problem Led to System Failure at Dhahran, Saudi Arabia reported on the cause of the failure. It turns out that the cause was an inaccurate calculation of the time since boot due to computer arithmetic errors.

The computer used to control the Patriot missile is based on a 1970s design and uses 24-bit arithmetic. The Patriot system tracks its target by measuring the time it takes for radar pulses to bounce back from them. Time is recorded by the system clock in tenths of a second, but is stored as an integer. To enable tracking calculations the time is converted to a 24-bit floating point number.

Rounding errors in the time conversions cause shifts in the system's "range gate", which is used to track the target.

Julio Mulero, professor of Mathematics at the University of Alicante explains that neither the algorithms nor the computers failed, but simply "a tiny error of "0.000000095 seconds" was ignored. It is a binary error equivalent to 0.000000095 seconds, but the problem is that the computers had been running for 100 hours. 100 hours is 3,600,000 tenths of a second. If we apply an error of 0.000000095 seconds to each tenth, the total error is 0.342 seconds.

The consequences were very large, causing the death of 28 soldiers and injuring 100 people. [67][68]

Chapter 5:

MEDICAL ERROR STORIES

The Therac-25 machine.

The Therac-25 was a machine built to give radiation treatments to cancer patients. Most of these patients had already undergone surgery to remove most of the tumor, the patients were usually given a series of low-energy radiation treatments to gradually and safely remove any remaining cancerous growth. This high-energy radiation machine was computer-controlled and cost millions of dollars.

In 1986, one of the patients went to the clinic for his usual radiation treatment. The technician mistakenly entered an "x" into the computer, which stood for X-ray beam, and immediately he realized the error, changed the "x" to an "e" for electron beam, and pressed "enter" showing the machine that they were ready to begin treatment. The computer gave the "beam ready" signal, and the technician pressed "b" to deliver the beam to the patient. But then the computer responded with an error message. Usually, this message meant that the treatment had not been performed. So the technician repeated the process a second time, and again there was an error message. From the other side the patient began to feel severe stabbing pains in his back, which was very different from his usual treatments, and he withdrew after three shocking attempts.

As the commands were changed in such a short time, the computer was not responding properly, and an overdose was administered that was more than 125 times the normal dose. Ray's health deteriorated rapidly, and he died 4 months later from complications of significant radiation burns. Unfortunately, six accidents involving significant overdoses of radiation to patients resulting in death occurred between 1985 and 1987. Summarizing the factors that produced this sad event, and according to the article "An Investigation of the Therac-25 Accidents" by authors Nancy Levenson and Clark S. Turner, the basic mistakes that were made in this case were poor software engineering practices, coding errors, general unsafe software design, insufficient testing, and an inadequate reporting system. [69][70]

Up to 270 women may have died due an algorithm bug.

In a somber turn of events, Jeremy Hunt, a former UK Health Secretary, extended an apology that reflected the weight of his position. His words held a sincere tone as he expressed, "Tragically, there are likely to be some people in this group who would have been alive today if this failure had not happened."

Hunt's grave words refer to an algorithmic bug that cast its shadow over the lives of up to 270 women in England. Their absence from the final rounds of routine breast cancer screenings, owing to invitations that never arrived, was a cause for strong concern. Within the fold of this narrative, nearly 450,000 women aged between 68 and 71 were inadvertently denied these invitations since the start of 2009. Amidst this revelation, Hunt commenced an independent review, coupled with his heartfelt apology to the affected women and their families. This ill-fated turn of events, he explained, could be traced back to a computational algorithm gone awry.

Within the precincts of the United Kingdom, women aged 50 to 70 are delivered automatic invitations to participate in breast cancer screening procedures every three years. This strategic timeline correlates with the progressive odds of encountering breast cancer as age advances. Nonetheless, the causal relationship between these delays in diagnosis and the potential for avoidable harm or mortality remains enshrouded in uncertainty. However, calculations based on estimates suggest a disheartening reality: the lifespans of 135 to 270 women may have abbreviated due to this distressing error.

Seeking resolution amidst the gloom, the government rectified the error within the algorithm and sought to make amends. Those afflicted – a cohort comprising 309,000 women who are still believed to be living – are to receive belated invitations for these essential screenings.

In a gesture acknowledging the profound disquiet these revelations might evoke, health officials have assumed the duty of reaching out to the next of kin of women who are believed to have fallen victim to this oversight, succumbing to breast cancer. In a gesture both noble and daunting, officials aim to extend their heartfelt apologies while concurrently initiating a somber evaluation to determine whether the deficiency in screening invitations precipitated untimely demises, which could potentially necessitate compensation. Acknowledging the emotional toll such a process might entail, Hunt solemnly intoned, "We are acutely aware that these circumstances will undoubtedly inflict immense distress upon some families." [71][72][73]

87

Chapter 6:

FINANCIAL ERROR STORIES

88

HSBC payments glitch.

The Hongkong and Shanghai Banking Corporation, or HSBC, is one of the largest and oldest financial institutions in the world. Founded in 1865 in Hong Kong and Shanghai, the bank has grown to become a global entity that offers a wide range of financial services to individuals, businesses, and institutions worldwide.

HSBC operates in over 60 countries and territories, providing banking, financial, and investment services that encompass personal and commercial banking, wealth management, investment banking, insurance, and more. The bank's international presence enables it to cater to a diverse customer base, ranging from individuals to large corporations.

The bank has faced a series of challenges and criticisms over the years. In particular, one of the challenges came in the form of a software error that impacted approximately 275,000 Bacs payments, leaving thousands of customers without their monthly salaries just before a bank holiday. Bacs is the system through which British banks handle the processing of countless direct debits and direct credits. HSBC stated that the issue stemmed from a flaw in the data contained within a file submitted to Bacs on Thursday night. Below, I outline how this error impacted the lives of several families:

• A senior content and online PR manager from Harrogate, who was scheduled to be married in May 2016, shared with The Guardian that the bank's issues might have jeopardized her wedding plans.

• A digital marketing specialist who works in sales encountered salary payment issues due to his employer's affiliation with HSBC. Facing a concerning situation, he expressed his distress at waking up to discover he lacked the necessary funds to cover the rental deposit for an upcoming move to a new flat scheduled for the next day.

• An individual operating an IT services business in London reported that none of his 130 employees had received their salaries. Despite initiating the necessary actions for payments a few days prior and anticipating HSBC's cooperation, the disheartening reality unfolded at around 7:30 a.m. on Friday morning when it became evident that none of the staff members had received their funds.

HSBC has issued an apology for the inconvenience caused and assured a prompt resolution of the matter. However, a definite timeline for this resolution remained uncertain. Customers were advised to refer to HSBC's Twitter account for real-time updates. Predictably, most customers expressed their frustration with the situation.

In general, the situation had a negative impact on HSBC's reputation in terms of customer satisfaction, costs, and regulatory perception. Recovery required efforts to address the current issues and strengthen the infrastructure and practices to prevent future disruptions. [74][75][76]

PayPal accidentally credits man $92 quadrillion.

In 2013, a Pennsylvania man received an unexpected surprise when he logged into his PayPal account and discovered that his balance had been credited with an eye-popping $92 quadrillion (that's 92 followed by 15 zeros). To put that in perspective, the world's gross domestic product at the time was estimated to be around $71 trillion. That means this person's PayPal balance was more than 1,000 times larger than the entire global economy.

The reason for the massive credit was a software bug that occurred during a routine test of PayPal's systems. The bug caused an error in the system, generating a transaction that credited this account with the absurdly large sum of money.

While this man initially thought the credit was a prank, he soon realized that it was legitimate when he received an email from PayPal confirming the transaction. The PayPal account was not linked to any bank account, so he was not able to withdraw any of the money or use it to make purchases.

The incident quickly gained international attention, with news outlets around the world reporting on the story. While the mistake was certainly amusing, it also highlighted the potential risks and challenges involved in the world of online transactions, showing that even small errors or glitches in software can have significant consequences, particularly when it comes to financial transactions. In response to the incident, PayPal quickly corrected the error and credited Reynolds' account with the correct balance. The company also issued a statement apologizing for the error and reassuring customers that their accounts were safe and secure.

The incident raised serious questions about the reliability and security of online payment systems. While services like PayPal offer convenience and flexibility to consumers, they also require a high degree of trust in the systems and companies that manage them.

Ultimately, the PayPal incident serves as a reminder of the importance of robust software testing and quality assurance in the development of online payment systems. As technology continues to advance and the world becomes increasingly interconnected, the need for secure and reliable online transactions will only continue to grow. [77][78][79]

Chapter 7:

AUTOMOTIVE ERROR STORIES

94

Toyota Prius recalled over software glitch.

In February 2014, Toyota announced a recall of approximately 1.9 million Prius vehicles worldwide due to a software glitch that could cause the car to stall unexpectedly. The recall affected third-generation Prius models produced between 2010 and 2014, which accounted for 713,000 vehicles in North America, 997,000 in Japan, 130,000 in Europe, and 18,000 in China.

The issue stemmed from a software malfunction within the car's hybrid system that damaged transistors and triggered warning lights. This led to a decrease in driving power and could even stop the vehicle completely. Fortunately, there were no reports of accidents or injuries associated with this software glitch.

Toyota said it had identified the problem during routine testing but had received no reports from customers about the issue. The company vowed to update the software in affected vehicles free of charge, which involved updating the car's motor control ECU software to eliminate the bug.

The recall was not the first for the Prius. In 2010, Toyota recalled approximately 500,000 Prius vehicles globally due to a software problem that could cause the brakes to fail, according to reports from customers in Japan and the US. In that case, the company said the software glitch could cause a brief delay in the car's braking system but that it was not a safety issue.

The recalls were a setback for Toyota, which has built a reputation for producing reliable and safe vehicles, but the company was already facing a number of lawsuits related to accidents allegedly caused by unintended acceleration in its vehicles. In 2010, Toyota recalled more than eight million vehicles worldwide due to reports of unintended acceleration, which was blamed for several accidents and deaths. The company agreed to pay $1.2 billion to settle a U.S. Department of Justice investigation into the issue in 2014.

The Prius recall was part of a larger trend in the automotive industry, which has seen an increasing reliance on software and computer systems to control and monitor vehicle performance. This has led to a few software-related problems and recalls in recent years, as automakers have struggled to keep pace with advances in technology and address the growing number of software vulnerabilities in their vehicles. [80][81]

Memory Failure - Tesla Recalls 135,000 Vehicle.

In June 2021, Tesla announced a recall of approximately 135,000 vehicles due to a software bug related to the memory in the vehicles' media control units (MCUs). The recall affected Model S and Model X vehicles built before March 2018 that were equipped with an NVIDIA Tegra 3 processor and an 8GB eMMC NAND flash memory chip.

The problem began when Tesla owners started experiencing issues with their vehicles' touchscreen displays. When the touchscreen's flash memory reached the end of its useful life, it "can cause failures of the center display software components and may indirectly cause loss of the rearview camera display, defrost/defog control settings and exterior turn signal lighting," the manufacturer said.

Upon investigation, Tesla determined that the root cause of the problem was a memory failure in the media control unit, which was caused by excessive data logging. The MCU was constantly writing data to the NAND memory, eventually causing it to wear out and fail, leading to touchscreen display issues. Tesla initially tried to address the problem with a software update that would have reduced the amount of data logging and extended the life of the unit's memory. However, it was determined that hardware replacement was necessary to fully resolve the issue.

The recall required affected owners to bring their vehicles to a Tesla service center so that the media control unit could be replaced. With Tesla performing the repairs free of charge, the recall represented a significant logistical challenge for the company. Over 135,000 vehicles were affected, making the recall one of the largest in Tesla's history.

The recall highlighted the increasing importance of software in modern vehicles, as many of the functions in the affected Tesla models were controlled through the MCU. It also raised concerns about the security of data collected by vehicles, as the excessive data logging that caused the memory failure was related to vehicle telemetry and diagnostic information.

Overall, the recall was a significant setback for Tesla, as it affected a large number of vehicles and required significant resources to resolve. However, the company's quick response and commitment to addressing the issue helped to mitigate the impact on affected owners and maintain trust in the brand. [82][83][84][85]

Chapter 8:

ACESSIBILITY ERROR STORIES

Beyoncé's Parkwood Entertainment settles lawsuit over website due accessibility issues.

In 2019, Parkwood Entertainment, Beyoncé's management company, was sued for violating the Americans with Disabilities Act (ADA) by a visually impaired woman named Mary Conner. Conner argued that the singer's official website (Beyonce.com) was inaccessible to visually impaired people due to some accessibility issues, lack of labels on buttons and images, as well as the lack of compatibility with screen-reading software.

The lawsuit alleged that this was discriminatory and violated Title III of the ADA, which requires businesses to provide equal access to their services for people with disabilities. The lawsuit sought a court order for the website to be modified to be accessible for people with visual disabilities, as well as seeking damages and legal costs.

In 2021, Beyoncé and Parkwood Entertainment reached a settlement with

Conner. The terms of the settlement were not publicly disclosed, but Beyoncé agreed to take several measures to improve the website's accessibility. This included changes to the website to improve accessibility, such as proper labels for buttons and images, compatibility with screen-reading software, and alternative text for non-textual elements.

Additionally, Beyoncé agreed to regularly test the website's accessibility, develop an accessibility policy, and provide training to employees and contractors involved in the design, development, and maintenance of the website. She also committed to reporting on progress in improving accessibility and providing regular updates to Conner.

This case highlights the importance of online accessibility and how businesses must take steps to improve it. Online accessibility is vital to ensure that all people, regardless of their abilities, have access to the online services they need. This case also highlights the need to comply with the Americans with Disabilities Act and how this law can protect the rights of people with disabilities. [86][87][88]

NAD's Lawsuit Against Harvard and MIT.

In 2015, the National Association of the Deaf (NAD) filed a lawsuit against Harvard University and the Massachusetts Institute of Technology (MIT) for not providing closed captions for their online course materials. The NAD argued that the universities were violating the Americans with Disabilities Act, which prohibits discrimination against individuals with disabilities in all areas of public life.

The lawsuit claimed that the online course materials, including lectures, videos, and other content, were not accessible to individuals who are deaf or hard of hearing because they did not include closed captions. The NAD argued that the lack of closed captions made it difficult or impossible for such individuals to fully participate in the courses and access the educational materials. Harvard and MIT both defended their position, stating that they had made significant efforts to make their online course materials accessible, including providing transcripts and other written materials. However, the NAD argued that these efforts were not sufficient and that the universities had a legal obligation to provide closed captions as well.

The lawsuit garnered significant attention and sparked a larger discussion about the accessibility of online content. Many disability rights advocates argued that the lack of closed captions and other accessibility features on online platforms is a widespread problem that needs to be addressed.

In the end, both Harvard and MIT settled the lawsuit with the NAD. Under the terms of the settlement, the universities agreed to provide closed captions for all online course materials as well as other accessibility features for individuals with disabilities. The settlement was seen as a significant victory for disability rights advocates and a step toward greater accessibility in online education. [89][90][91]

Domino's Pizza Settles Lawsuit Over Inaccessible Website.

In 2016, a blind customer named Guillermo Robles sued Domino's Pizza for violating the Americans with Disabilities Act by having an inaccessible website and mobile app. Robles claimed that he was unable to order pizza online or using the mobile app because neither the website nor app were compatible with his screen-reader software.

Despite Apple's smartphones incorporating screen-reading software to help their visually impaired owners use the Internet, the software relies on alternative text contained within images and other visual elements to function properly, and these were missing from Domino's site.

Attorneys for Robles argued in court papers that the Americans with Disabilities Act requires businesses with physical locations to make their websites and other online platforms accessible to those with disabilities. The district court dismissed the case, and Robles' appeal sent him to the Ninth Circuit Court of Appeals, which ruled in his favor. The panel sided with Robles, writing that the "alleged inaccessibility of Domino's website and app impedes access to the goods and services of its physical pizza franchises – which are places of public accommodation."

Domino's rejected Robles' claim that Title III of the Americans with Disabilities Act covers mobile apps or websites, which did not actually exist in their modern forms when the ADA was passed in 1990. They also contended that there were no clear guidelines on how to make their digital platforms accessible. Robles argued that the ADA does cover the web and software, as long as the company has physical locations in the U.S. and solicits customers over the Internet. Thus, Domino's requested the Supreme Court to review the appellate court's decision. However, the court declined to do so, which meant that Domino's would have to contest Robles' inaccessibility claims in court.

Subsequently, on June 23, 2021, the Central District Court of California granted the plaintiff's motion and ruled that Domino's had violated Title III by not providing a fully accessible website. The court's ruling stated that, although a website is not a place of public accommodation, an inaccessible website impedes access to the goods and services of its physical pizza franchises, which are places of public accommodation. As a result, the court ordered Domino's to bring its website in compliance with WCAG 2.0 standards.

Following several years of litigation, on June 6, 2022, both parties filed a notice of settlement, effectively ending the legal dispute. [92][93][94]

Lawsuit against Winn-Dixie.

In 2017, a historic lawsuit was brought against the Florida-based supermarket chain Winn-Dixie in the District Court for the Southern District of Florida by plaintiff Juan Carlos Gil. This marked the first-ever ADA website case to go to trial, setting a significant legal precedent. Interestingly, at the time of the suit, Winn-Dixie did not use its website to sell groceries or any other merchandise. Rather, the site provided a number of key functions that Gil, who is visually impaired, wanted to use.

These included the ability to locate Winn-Dixie stores, to link digital coupons to user rewards cards for use in-store, and to make prescription refill requests for in-store pickup.

For Gil, the prescription refill function was particularly appealing because it allowed him to maintain his privacy during sensitive conversations with the pharmacist while also avoiding lengthy in-person wait times. However, the website presented significant accessibility barriers, including the lack of alternative text descriptions for images, a lack of compatibility with assistive technology for reading aloud, and the absence of a virtual keyboard to navigate the site without a mouse.

On April 7, 2021, the Eleventh Circuit Court of Appeals issued a decision that overturned the district court's ruling in the Winn-Dixie case. The court held that websites do not qualify as places of public accommodation under Title III of the ADA, which is limited to "actual, physical places." The court clarified that the ADA may still apply to websites that function as an extension of physical spaces. However, it concluded that Winn-Dixie's website did not meet this standard.

The court noted that the Winn-Dixie website only had limited functionality and was not a point of sale, as all purchases must occur in-store. Additionally, any interactions with the grocery store that can be initiated on the website must be completed in-person at a physical store location. The court further stated that, while the plaintiff, Juan Carlos Gil, may not have always been satisfied with the speed or privacy of service he received at the pharmacy, he was not prevented from refilling his prescriptions as a Winn-Dixie customer. [95][96][97]

Chapter 9:

PERFORMANCE ERROR STORIES

Disney+ fell on the day of its launch.

As the launch of Disney+ approached, anticipation was high among fans of the beloved entertainment company. However, as fate would have it, things didn't quite go according to plan. The hashtag #DisneyPlusFail quickly began to trend on Twitter, with thousands of users reporting that the service was not working as of the first afternoon. One error screen displayed Mickey Mouse and Pluto wearing spacesuits, accompanied by the text: "We are having a problem. Please exit the app and try again."

And, as always, Twitter was witness to the emotions of Disney+ users who tweeted their thoughts – some funny, some rude, some philosophical, and even conspiratorial. Another screen showed Ralph and Vanellope from Wreck-It Ralph below a tweet that read: "At least the Disney+ error screens are fun." Another twitter user posted: "Just like your parks, you weren't ready for the traffic." Another comment from that day was: "The brand name that [they are] going to get tagged with if they don't get this cleared up quickly is Disney Minus," But what happened to Disney+ on the day of its launch? Some of the issues that were reported on the first day included:

• Server overload: The high volume of users attempting to access the service caused an overload on the servers, leading to crashes and slow loading times.

• Sign-in issues: Some users reported difficulty signing in to their accounts, either due to technical issues or incorrect login information.

• Video playback problems: A number of users experienced issues with video playback, including buffering, freezing, and poor quality.

• Search functionality problems: Some users reported issues with the search function, including slow loading times and inaccurate results.

Disney+ spokesman Kevin Mayer attributed the problem to a high user turnout that "exceeded the highest expectations." According to Mayer: "It's literally one part of the tech stack that we use in a certain way that we should use another way… It had to do with the way we architected a piece of the app… It was a coding issue, and we're going to recode it." Disney+ may have fallen victim to its own promotional campaign by not foreseeing this avalanche of users desperate to access the streaming platform.

On the other hand – without getting into conspiracy theories and instead just talking about investment strategies – Disney+ could have prepared its architecture to support this flood of simultaneous users, but it probably would not have been as cost-effective as fixing the problems on the fly. With an overview of what actually happened, they could have adjusted their technology architecture based on the expected high demand.

Disney+ experienced a lot of problems on its launch day due to the high number of people who tried to use the service. This caused the servers to crash, and many users had trouble accessing their accounts or watching videos. It was a big disappointment for fans who were eagerly anticipating the launch. It's important for companies like Disney+ to anticipate the impact of a large number of users and prepare their technology architecture to support the demand. This will help prevent future problems and keep their customers happy. [98][99][100]

Cute Dog Photos due to the fall of Amazon Prime.

In 2018, Amazon Prime Day was set to be the largest online shopping event of the year, providing customers with exclusive deals and discounts on a broad range of products. However, what should have been a record-breaking day quickly turned into a nightmare for the e-commerce giant, as it faced significant performance issues.

The trouble began early in the morning, as customers from all over the world rushed to the Amazon website to take advantage of the offers. Within minutes, the site began experiencing slowdowns and crashes, making it impossible for customers to browse or make purchases. Some customers received error messages, while others discovered that items in their carts were suddenly out of stock. However, Amazon managed to keep its customers amused by displaying cute pictures of puppies.

As the hours went by, the situation worsened. Customers took to social media to express their frustration and anger, with many declaring that they would never shop on Amazon again. The hashtag #PrimeDayFail began trending on Twitter.

According to CNBC, Amazon was unable to secure enough servers to handle the massive influx of simultaneous users on Prime Day. To address the performance issues experienced that day, Amazon had to manually add servers, indicating that its auto-scaling feature may not have worked as expected leading up to the crash. The outage not only affected Amazon's e-commerce site but also its voice-operated assistant, Alexa, and streaming platform, Twitch, which experienced functionality problems. Furthermore, some of Amazon's warehouses were unable to scan or package orders.

As a result of this array of errors, Amazon switched to a simpler "fallback" page. The Prime Day homepage appeared oddly simple and somewhat poorly designed, indicating that Amazon had sought a simplified homepage to reduce the load on its servers. Amazon also temporarily halted all international traffic to "reduce the pressure" on its Sable system.

Despite the performance issues experienced during Prime Day, Amazon has continued to improve its website and infrastructure to prevent similar incidents from occurring in the future. The company has invested significantly in new technology and infrastructure to improve website performance and increase capacity. Additionally, Amazon has implemented new measures to enhance the reliability and scalability of its systems, including a new auto-scaling feature that automatically adds or removes server capacity as required. Although the Prime Day outage was a significant setback, Amazon has used the experience as a learning opportunity to improve and strengthen its e-commerce platform. [101][102][103]

HealthCare.gov went down.

The Affordable Care Act, which aimed to increase healthcare access for all Americans, was signed into law by President Obama on March 23, 2010. As part of this legislation, the United States Department of Health and Human Services (HHS) was required to launch HealthCare.gov to help people enroll in insurance plans, which they did in October 2013.

The Affordable Care Act allowed states to establish their own healthcare exchange or participate in the federal exchange. However, the launch of the website was a complete failure.

Almost immediately, users began reporting errors and crashes, making it impossible for them to enroll in insurance plans. The website was slow, unresponsive, and frequently displayed error messages. Many users were unable to even create accounts or log in. The problems were so severe that the government was forced to extend the enrollment period, which had a significant impact on the implementation of the Affordable Care Act.

According to administration officials, the federal website was unexpectedly inundated with 2.8 million visitors, far surpassing their projections. As a result, website technicians at the Department of Health and Human Services were forced to launch an all-out response to address the overwhelming demand. White House senior adviser David Simas acknowledged that, while they had anticipated a gradual increase in traffic, the response on launch day was beyond what they had anticipated, even exceeding the traffic experienced during a typical day for Medicare. Simas remained optimistic, however, stating that the identified problems would be addressed and resolved to improve performance for the following day.

"That gives you a sense of how important this is to millions of Americans around the country, and that's a good thing," President Obama said. "We're going to be speeding things up in the next few hours to handle all of this demand that exceeds anything that we had expected."

Harvard University's website states that there were three root causes for the failed launch of HealthCare.gov: lack of relevant experience, lack of leadership, and schedule pressure. HHS employees and managers lacked experience in technology product launches, technical positions were unfilled, and project managers had little knowledge of the required work. There was no formal division of responsibilities, causing delays in key decision-making and communication issues. Finally, the mandated launch date created schedule pressure, and HHS employees were forced to launch the website on time regardless of completion or the amount of testing and troubleshooting performed.

While government initiatives aimed at providing valuable civic services are essential, it is crucial to consider the technological challenges associated with launching websites to manage these initiatives. The impact of web performance cannot be underestimated, especially when these initiatives attract a large number of users seeking vital services that impact their daily lives. [104][105][106]

Taylor Swift's "Midnights" album crashes Spotify.

In October 2022, Taylor Swift released her album Midnights on various music streaming platforms, including Spotify. The album quickly gained immense popularity among her fans, causing a surge in traffic on the Spotify platform. Numerous Spotify users reported frequent app crashes and difficulty accessing their subscriptions on both Android and iOS. Additionally, some users experienced app malfunctions despite seemingly having an internet connection, leading them to speculate that there may have been an issue with their connection.

Spotify faced more than 8,000 outages due to the high traffic caused by Taylor Swift's album. This was an unprecedented event, as the album broke the record for the most streams in a day on the platform – 228 million. The previous record was 153 million streams, making it clear that the album was a massive success despite the initial technical challenges.

Reports of Spotify crashing came in just minutes after the release of Midnights, causing Swifties to take to Twitter to express their grievances. Some of those tweets are as follows:

• Spotify crashed following the release of Taylor Swift's new album #Midnights

• why must taylor swift crash Spotify during every album release

• did taylor swift just crash spotify

What is certain is that Spotify dealt with real consequences. Spotify operates on a subscription model and also earns revenue from ads. The technical glitch during the launch of Taylor Swift's album caused the platform to lose both ad revenue and users' trust. However, the incident generated a lot of attention and publicity for Swift, which was a positive outcome for her.

Did Taylor Swift's 2022 album release cause Spotify to crash? Some people think so, citing the album's subliminal messages. For example, the single "Anti-Hero" features the line "It's me, hi, I'm the problem, it's me," which could be interpreted as foreshadowing to the incident. Of course, this is just a humorous perspective. What do you think about the album's impact on Spotify, if any? [107] [108] [109] [110]

Chapter 10:

USABILITY ERROR STORIES

Snapchat's Redesign, usability glitches.

Snapchat is a mobile application that allows users to share photos and videos that disappear after a set amount of time. What makes Snapchat particularly popular among younger users is its fun and interactive features, such as the ability to add filters, text, and drawings to posts.

With the aim of improving user experience, Snapchat made some changes in 2018 that affected the usability of the application. The major redesign was meant to simplify its interface and make the app more user-friendly. However, the changes drew significant criticism from users, who found the new layout confusing and difficult to navigate. The app's redesign was intended to attract a wider range of users and expand Snapchat's user base. However, the changes were so drastic that many Snapchat users were unprepared and struggled to adjust to the new design, which did not have the effect that Snap had intended.

Despite the backlash and calls to revert to the old design, Snapchat chose to proceed with its new format. This decision disappointed many users who found the redesign frustrating and confusing. One of the most criticized aspects of the new design was the separation of social media content from publisher content. Previously, users could view posts from friends, content creators, and publishers in a single feed. However, the new design separated these elements, which blurred the line between friends and content creators.

The redesign also eliminated the Stories page within the app, which was a popular feature among Snapchat's users. Instead, user posts and messages were moved to one section, while publisher content was placed in a separate section. Snapchat's goal was to reduce the pressure users felt when posting on the platform by lowering the bar for what is considered worthy content.

However, many users found the new format – meant to simplify the app – more complicated and harder to use than the previous one. As a result, many users have expressed frustration and resorted to risky measures such as using VPN apps or taking other steps to revert to the previous version of Snapchat. The new features introduced in the update have been criticized as useless and deviating from Snapchat's original purpose, which had been consistent for several years. Numerous users voiced their concerns about its usability. More than a million people signed an online petition on Change.org titled "Remove the New Snapchat Update," calling on Snapchat to reverse its update and revert to the original design.

Twitter was home to an avalanche of users unhappy with these changes due to flaws in the usability of the application. Celebrities and influencers used the little blue bird to demonstrate their dissatisfaction, including influencer and popular star Kylie Jenner, who tweeted that she hadn't been using the app that much and called the changes "sad." A complaint on Twitter about Snapchat's redesign became one of the most retweeted messages of all time.

Snap confirmed that the redesign lost two percent of its daily active users, which dropped from 191 million to 188 million in just a quarter. [111][112][113]

Windows 8 Start Screen - In 2012.

When Microsoft introduced the Windows 8 operating system, its new Start screen was criticized by users for being confusing and difficult to navigate. The company later made changes to the design in response to user feedback. Launched in 2012, Windows 8 was Microsoft's successor to Windows 7 and was meant to revolutionize the user experience.

Departing from the conventional Windows UI, this version placed a significant emphasis on touch-friendly interface components, notably introducing the dynamic Start screen. At its core, Windows 8 aspired to usher in the next phase of Windows evolution. This transformation aimed to reshape the operating system from being primarily desktop-centric to one seamlessly adaptable to both desktop and tablet environments, ensuring a harmonious user experience across platforms.

Windows 8's shortcomings stemmed from a combination of design and usability issues. Ranging from a poorly executed UI design to the inexplicable removal of essential features such as the Start Button, Microsoft notably fumbled its execution of the 2012 operating system.

The Nielsen Norman Group conducted a usability evaluation led by Jacob Nielsen, one of the most recognized experts in usability worldwide. To ascertain actual user performance, they invited 12 experienced PC users to test Windows 8 on both conventional computers and Microsoft's new Surface RT tablets.

At first glance, the system presents two facets to the user: a tablet-oriented Start screen and a PC-oriented desktop screen. Unfortunately, including dual environments on a single device is a recipe for usability issues for several reasons, as users must learn and remember where to navigate for specific functions, resulting in an inconsistent user experience.

Another notable aspect of Windows 8 for advanced users is that the product's name itself has become misleading. The Windows system no longer supports multiple windows on the screen. While Windows 8 includes an option to temporarily display a secondary area on a small part of the screen, none of the users found this to function properly.

It was evident that users didn't mind horizontal scrolling on the Surface, which is intriguing considering that horizontal scrolling is a usability disaster for desktop websites. Nonetheless, there is a concept called "scroll overload," which posits that users won't invest time navigating through large quantities of low-density information.

Many other Windows 8 features were initially concealed and only revealed when users perform specific, often intricate gestures. For instance, users encountered significant difficulties with an exceedingly basic task: altering the city in the system's weather application. Obvious gestures, like clicking on the current city's name to change location, proved ineffective. User challenges were exacerbated by the modern graphical user interface (GUI) style's failure to indicate active words and fields.

This analysis should serve as a wake-up call to software developers, reminding them that usability is not a secondary feature but a fundamental cornerstone for product design and development. Empathy for users and continual iteration are essential to crafting solutions that are intuitive and efficient. By comprehending how design decisions can impact user interaction, developers can ensure their products are valuable and appealing to a broader audience. [114][115][116]

Awful lot of bugs still…

126

REFERENCE

[1]: The Edison Historic Homes SEMINOLE LODGE
https://www.edisonfordwinterestates.org/

[2]: Thomas Alva Edison; sixty years of an inventor's life. By Jones, Francis Arthur.
1908. Pag. 250.
https://archive.org/details/thomasalvaedison00jonerich/page/250/mode/2up

[3] Letter from Thomas Alva Edison to William Orton, March 3rd,
1878. https://edisondigital.rutgers.edu/document/X099AT

[4] Letter from Thomas Alva Edison to Theodore Puskas, November 13th, 1878.
https://edisondigital.rutgers.edu/document/LB003487

[5] The Papers of Thomas A. Edison: From Workshop to Laboratory, June 1873-
March 1876. by Nier, Keith, Israel, Paul B., Edison, Thomas A. Pag 4, 21, 22, 24,
217, 219, 229.

[6]: Smithsonian Libraries and Archives - Digital Library. The Operator. The
telegraph operators' journal. Pags, 5, 8, 10. Vol III, Mar, 1, 1975.
https://archive.org/details/operator03newy/page/n7/mode/2up

[7]: The standard electrical dictionary, by Sloane, T. O'Conor (Thomas O'Conor).
1982.Pag. 92.
https://archive.org/details/standardelectri00sloagoog/page/92/mode/2up

[8]: The Monitor. January 1924. Pag. 14, 34.
https://bh.hallikainen.org/thg/monitor/Monitor_1924-01.pdf

[9] The Internet Pinball Database: Baffle Ball. Designed by David Gottlieb.
November, 1931. https://www.ipdb.org/showpic.pl?id=129&picno=16257

[10] Life magazine. "Modern Aircraft Carriers are Result of 20 Years of Smart
Experimentation. June 29th, 1942.
https://books.google.com/books?id=KlAEAAAAMBAJ

[11] We Took to the Woods. 1942. Louise Dickinson Rich.

[12] National Museum of American History. Log Book With Computer Bug.
https://americanhistory.si.edu/collections/search/object/nmah_334663

[13]: What Happened on September 9th.

https://www.computerhistory.org/tdih/september/9/

[14]: Smithsonian Honors the Original Bug in the System. New York Time. Peter Wayner.
https://archive.nytimes.com/www.nytimes.com/library/cyber/week/120497bug.html

[15]. Electronic Numerical Integrator and Computer. 1999. Scott McCartney.

[16] The Internet Worm Incident. Eugene H. Spafford.
https://docs.lib.purdue.edu/cgi/viewcontent.cgi?article=1792&context=cstech

[17] With Microscope and tweezers: An Analysis of the Internet Virus of November 1988. Mark W, Eichin and Jon A. Rochlis.
https://course.ece.cmu.edu/~ece845/docs/eichin.pdf

[18] Almost a Tragedy: The Collapse of the Hartford Civic Center. Ben Gammell.
https://connecticuthistory.org/almost-a-tragedy-the-collapse-of-the-hartford-civic-center/

[19] Coliseum Roof Collapses at Hartford Civic Center. Lawrence Fellows.
https://www.nytimes.com/1978/01/19/archives/coliseum-roof-collapses-at-hartford-civic-center-coliseum-roof.html

[20] Flaw in Kerberos System Corrected. Dan McGuire.
http://tech.mit.edu/V116/N11/kerberos.11n.html

[21] Misplaced T Misplaced Trust: Kerberos 4 Session. Bryan Dole, Steve Lodin, Eugene H. Spafford.
https://docs.lib.purdue.edu/cgi/viewcontent.cgi?article=2331&context=cstech

[22] The Crash of the AT&T Network in 1990. Peter G. Neumann.
https://telephoneworld.org/landline-telephone-history/the-crash-of-the-att-network-in-1990/

[23] Massachusetts Institute of Technology.
http://www.mit.edu/hacker/part1.html

[24] Risk Analysis of the Pentium Bug. Vaughan Pratt.
http://boole.stanford.edu/pentium.html

[25] Pentium Division Bug. United States Naval Academy.
https://www.usna.edu/Users/cs/lmcdowel/courses/ic220/S20/projects/courseP

aper/sample.pdf

[26] The Pentium FDIV Bug. Northeastern University. https://course.khoury.northeastern.edu/cs5500f14/Notes/Testing2/FDIVbug.html

[27] Is the Year 2038 problem the new Y2K bug? Samuel Gibbs. https://www.theguardian.com/technology/2014/dec/17/is-the-year-2038-problem-the-new-y2k-bug

[28] Early Year 2000 glitches provide sneak preview. Thomas Hoffman and Julia King. http://www.cnn.com/TECH/computing/9808/28/ y2k.preview

[29] Was Y2K bug a boost? Damian Carrington. http://news.bbc.co.uk/2/hi/science/nature/590932.stm

[30] 'Gangnam Style' breaks YouTube. Brandon Griggs. https://www.cnn.com/2014/12/03/showbiz/gangnam-style-youtube/index.html

[31] Psy's 'Gangnam Style' becomes most viewed YouTube video of all time. Louis Goddard. https://www.theverge.com/2012/11/24/3685210/gangnam-style-most-viewed-youtube

[32] August 2003 Blackout. Office of Electricity. https://www.energy.gov/oe/august-2003-blackout

[33] Blackout hits Northeast United States. This Day In History. https://www.history.com/this-day-in-history/blackout-hits-northeast-united-states

[34] The passport delays of Summer 1999. The United Kingdom Passport Agency. https://webarchive.nationalarchives.gov.uk/ukgwa/20170207052351/https://www.nao.org.uk/wp-content/uploads/1999/10/9899812.pdf

[35] UK: Wales Holidaymakers may foot bill for passport chaos. BBC NEWS. http://news.bbc.co.uk/2/hi/uk_news/wales/487351.stm

[36] Biggest Windows bloopers. David Goldman. https://money.cnn.com/galleries/2009/technology/0910/gallery.microsoft_windows_gaffes/index.html

[37] Windows 98 Crashes Live On Stage. On this day. https://freecontent.manning.com/on-this-day-04-20/

[38] Reebok runs into trouble over mistaken free trainers offer. Rebecca Smithers. https://www.theguardian.com/money/2013/nov/27/reebok-free-trainers-offer

[39] Shoppers rush to order FREE Reebok trainers worth £99.50 after website glitch meant they only paid the delivery charge of £8.50. HAYLEY O'KEEFFE. https://www.dailymail.co.uk/news/article-2513937/Shoppers-order-FREE-Reebok-trainers-website-glitch.html

[40] It's been 20 years since Windows 98 crashed live on stage with BSOD. Rakesh Singh. https://www.windowslatest.com/2018/04/25/its-been-20-years-since-windows-98-crashes-live-on-stage-with-bsod/

[41] Known Issues and Solutions. IRS. https://www.irs.gov/e-file-providers/known-issues-and-solutions

[42] Why you shouldn't take that IRS withholding calculator at face value. Darla Mercado. https://www.cnbc.com/2018/07/02/why-you-shouldnt-take-that-irs-withholding-calculator-at-face-value.html

[43] IRS payment site crashes hours before Tax Day filing deadline. Darla Mercado. https://www.cnbc.com/2018/04/17/irs-tax-payment-site-down-as-agency-works-to-resolve-issue.html

[44] Nest thermostat glitch battery dies software freeze. Nick Bilton. https://www.nytimes.com/2016/01/14/fashion/nest-thermostat-glitch-battery-dies-software-freeze.html

[45] Nest thermostat bug leaves users. Jane Wakefield. https://www.bbc.com/news/technology-35311447

[46] 'Flash freeze' halts Nasdaq stock trading for 3 hours. Patrick Rizzo. https://www.nbcnews.com/businessmain/flash-freeze-halts-nasdaq-stock-trading-3-hours-6c10974922

[47] Shutdown at Nasdaq Is Traced to Software. Michael J. De La Merced. https://archive.nytimes.com/dealbook.nytimes.com/2013/08/29/nasdaq-blames-a-surge-of-data-for-trading-halt/

[48] Nasdaq, NYSE play blame game over 'flash freeze'. Bob Pisani. https://www.cnbc.com/id/100992136

[49] Nasdaq takes blame for recent Flash Freeze. Matt Krantz. https://www.usatoday.com/story/money/markets/2013/08/29/nasdaq-blame-

flash-freeze/2728923/

[50] Mariner 1. National Aeronautics and Space Administration (NASA). https://nssdc.gsfc.nasa.gov/nmc/spacecraft/display.action?id=MARIN1

[51] Ariane 501 - Presentation of Inquiry Board Report . European Space Agency. https://www.esa.int/Newsroom/Press_Releases/Ariane_501_-_Presentation_of_Inquiry_Board_report

[52] ARIANE 5 Flight 501 Failure. J. L. Lions. http://sunnyday.mit.edu/nasa-class/Ariane5-report.html

[53] An analysis of the Ariane 5 flight 501 failure-a system engineering perspective. G. Le Lann. https://ieeexplore.ieee.org/document/581900

[54] Beyond Earth. A Chronicle Of Deep Space Exploration. Asif A. Siddiqi. https://www.nasa.gov/sites/default/files/atoms/files/beyond-earth-tagged.pdf

[55] Mars Climate Orbiter. National Aeronautics and Space Administration (NASA).]https://solarsystem.nasa.gov/missions/mars-climate-orbiter/in-depth/

[56] Mars Probe Lost Due to Simple Math Error. Robert Lee Hotz. https://www.latimes.com/archives/la-xpm-1999-oct-01-mn-17288-story.html

[57] Boeing astronaut capsule Starliner faces further delays as NASA investigation continues. Michael Sheetz. https://www.cnbc.com/2020/02/07/boeings-starliner-software-issues-under-nasa-investigation.html

[58] Boeing & NASA admit multiple anomalies on Starliner mission. Chris Gebhardt https://www.nasaspaceflight.com/2020/02/boeing-nasa-admit-multiple-anomalies-starliner-mission/

[59] Software maintenance mistake at center of major FAA computer meltdown. Sam Sweeney, Jon Haworth, Kevin Shalvey, Meredith Deliso, and Josh Margolin. https://abcnews.go.com/US/computer-failure-faa-impact-flights-nationwide/story?id=96358202

[60] Software: IT systems backup failure may be cause of FAA NOTAMS outage. ColdStreams. https://coldstreams.com/2023/01/12/software-maintenance-mistake-at-center-of-major-faa-computer-meltdown-official/

[61] American Airlines and others carriers were left helpless after a system outage crippled operations, causing delays. Thomas Pallini.

https://www.businessinsider.com/airlines-left-crippled-with-delays-after-sabre-system-outage-2021-5

[62] American Airlines sues Sabre over fare display. y Robert Silk. https://www.travelweekly.com/Travel-News/Airline-News/American-Airlines-sues-Sabre-over-fare-display

[63] Queen Opens London Heathrow's Terminal 5. CBS News. https://www.cbsnews.com/news/queen-opens-london-heathrows-terminal-5/

[64] The opening of Heathrow Terminal 5. House of Commons Transport Committee. https://publications.parliament.uk/pa/cm200708/cmselect/cmtran/543/543.pdf

[65] Had A Funny Feeling in My Gut. David Hoffman. https://www.washingtonpost.com/wp-srv/inatl/longterm/coldwar/shatter021099b.htm

[65] Film: The man who may have saved the world 2014. Director Peter Anthony. Casting: Stanislav Petrov, Kevin Costner, Sergey Shnyryov.

[67] The Patriot Missile Failure. Douglas N. Arnold. https://www-users.cse.umn.edu/~arnold/disasters/patriot.html

[68] Patriot Missile. Julio Mulero. https://mobile.twitter.com/juliomulero/status/1215314400892145665

[69] An investigation of the Therac-25 accidents Nancy G Leveson and Clark S. Turner. https://www.cs.columbia.edu/~junfeng/08fa-e6998/sched/readings/therac25.pdf

[70] An Engineering Disaster: Therac-25. Joanne Lim. https://tildesites.bowdoin.edu/~allen/courses/cs260/readings/therac.pdf

[71] Up to 270 women may have died after England breast cancer screening failures. Meera Senthilingam. https://www.cnn.com/2018/05/02/health/uk-breast-cancer-screening-scandal-intl/index.html

[72] Breast screening error 'shortened up to 270 lives' – Hunt. BBC. https://www.bbc.com/news/health-43973652

[73] How tech bugs could be killing thousands in our hospitals. Chris Baraniuk. https://www.newscientist.com/article/mg23831781-700-how-tech-bugs-could-be-

killing-thousands-in-our-hospitals/

[74] HSBC glitch payments 'all processed'. BBC. https://www.bbc.com/news/uk-34095626

[75] HSBC system failure leaves thousands facing bank holiday without pay. Lisa Bachelor and Patrick Collinson. https://www.theguardian.com/money/2015/aug/28/many-hsbc-customers-facing-payday-without-pay

[76] HSBC customers haven't been paid because of an IT glitch and they're furious. Ben Moshinsky. https://www.businessinsider.com/hsbc-customers-furious-at-pay-it-glitch-2015-8

[77] PayPal 'credits' US man $92 quadrillion in error. BBC. https://www.bbc.com/news/world-us-canada-23352230

[78] Oops! PayPal accidentally credits man $92 quadrillion. https://www.cnbc.com/id/100892381

[79] PayPal accidentally credits man $92 quadrillion. https://www.cnn.com/2013/07/17/tech/paypal-error/index.html

[80] Justice Department Announces Criminal Charge Against Toyota Motor Corporation and Deferred Prosecution Agreement with $1.2 Billion Financial Penalty. US Justice Department. https://www.justice.gov/opa/pr/justice-department-announces-criminal-charge-against-toyota-motor-corporation-and-deferred

[81] Toyota Recalls 1.9 Million Prius Vehicles Worldwide Over Glitch. Kimimasa Mayama. https://www.nbcnews.com/business/autos/toyota-recalls-1-9-million-prius-vehicles-worldwide-over-glitch-n28116

[82] Tesla Recalls 135,000 Model S, Model X Cars Over Touchscreen Failure. Jim Motavalli. https://www.forbes.com/wheels/news/tesla-recalls-135000-cars/

[83] Tesla recalls 135,000 cars after pushing back against regulators. Peter Valdes-Dapena. https://www.cnn.com/2021/02/02/business/tesla-screen-recall/index.html

[84] Tesla Will Recall 135,000 Cars for Faulty Touch Screens - The New York Times. Niraj Chokshi. https://www.nytimes.com/2021/02/02/business/tesla-recall.html

[85] Tesla to Recall 135,000 Vehicles Over Touchscreen Issue. Agence France-Presse. https://www.gadgets360.com/transportation/news/tesla-recall-car-135000-computer-touchscreen-issue-elon-musk-2362311

[86] Beyoncé's Parkwood Entertainment sued over website Accessibility. Laura Snapes https://www.theguardian.com/music/2019/jan/04/beyonce-parkwood-entertainment-sued-over-website-accessibility

[87] Beyonce's Parkwood Entertainment Sued Over Website Accessibility. Ashley Cullins. https://www.billboard.com/music/music-news/beyonce-parkwood-entertainment-sued-website-accessibility-8492195/

[88] Beyonce's Website the Focus of an Accessibility Lawsuit. Bureau of Internet Accessibility. https://www.boia.org/blog/beyonces-website-the-focus-of-an-accessibility-lawsuit

[89] NAD Sues Harvard and MIT for Discrimination in Public Online Content. National Association of the Deaf. https://www.nad.org/2015/02/17/nad-sues-harvard-and-mit-for-discrimination-in-public-online-content/

[90] NAD v Harvard Consent Decree. https://creeclaw.org/wp-content/uploads/2019/11/NAD-v-Harvard-Consent-Decree.pdf

[91] National Association of the Deaf v. Harvard and National Association of the Deaf v. MIThttps://creeclaw.org/case/online-content-lawsuit-harvard-mit/

[92] Dominos Petition. Supreme Court of the United States. https://www.supremecourt.gov/DocketPDF/18/181539/102950/201906131533 19483_DominosPetition.pdf

[93] The Robles v. Domino's Settlement (And Why It Matters). Bureau of Internet Accessibility. https://www.boia.org/blog/the-robles-v.-dominos-settlement-and-why-it-matters

[94] Supreme Court hands victory to blind man who sued Domino's over site accessibility. Tucker Higgins. https://www.cnbc.com/2019/10/07/dominos-supreme-court.html

[95] Lawyers Awarded $100K After Historic Verdict For Blind Internet Users; Winn-Dixie Appealing. John O'Brien. https://www.forbes.com/sites/legalnewsline/2017/10/02/lawyers-awarded-100k-after-historic-verdict-for-blind-internet-users-winn-dixie-

appealing/?sh=71f73ecf6b2e

[96] Gil V. Winn-Dixie Stores, Inc. Leagle.
https://www.leagle.com/decision/infdco20170614963

[97] 7 Accessibility FAQ on the Winn-Dixie ADA Appeal Decision (2021). Glenda
Sims. https://www.deque.com/blog/7-accessibility-questions-winn-dixie-ada-
appeal-decision/

[98] Disney+ suffers technical errors on launch day. Annie Palmer and Brandon
Gomez. https://www.cnbc.com/2019/11/12/disney-plus-experiences-errors-
connecting-on-launch-day.html

[99] Disney+ launch plagued with glitches on first day. Hana R. Alberts and
Alexandra Steigrad. https://nypost.com/2019/11/12/disney-streaming-service-
plagued-with-glitches-on-first-day/

[100] Disney+ launches, then crashes. Frank Pallotta.
https://www.cnn.com/2019/11/12/media/disney-error/index.html

[101] Why Amazon's Site Crashed on Prime Day. EMILY PRICE.
https://fortune.com/2018/07/20/amazon-crash-prime-day/

[102] Internal documents show how Amazon scrambled to fix Prime Day glitches.
Eugene Kim. https://www.cnbc.com/2018/07/19/amazon-internal-documents-
what-caused-prime-day-crash-company-scramble.html

[103] Amazon's likely multimillion-dollar disaster on Prime Day proved it's not
immune from embarrassment. Dennis Green.
https://www.businessinsider.com/amazon-prime-day-outage-most-embarrassing-
moment-retail-2018-12

[104] Healthcare.gov plagued by crashes on 1st day. Wyatt Andrews, Anna Werner.
https://www.cbsnews.com/news/healthcaregov-plagued-by-crashes-on-1st-day/

[105] The Failed Launch Of www.HealthCare.gov. Harvard University.
https://d3.harvard.edu/platform-rctom/submission/the-failed-launch-of-www-
healthcare-gov/

[106] Healthcare.gov: It Could Be Worse. Rusty Foster.
https://www.newyorker.com/tech/annals-of-technology/healthcare-gov-it-could-
be-worse

[107] Taylor Swift's 'Midnights' album crashes Spotify, leaving fans shocked; nearly 8,000 outages reported. y Stephanie Giang-Paunon. https://www.foxbusiness.com/entertainment/taylor-swifts-midnights-album-crashes-spotify-fans-shocked-8000-outages-reported

[108] Spotify crashes as Taylor Swift's hotly-anticipated 'Midnights' album launches. Nika Shakhnazarova. https://nypost.com/2022/10/21/taylor-swift-midnights-album-release-causes-spotify-outage/

[109] Taylor Swift fans fume as Spotify crashes as highly anticipated Midnights album launches. Daniel Bird and Jamie Roberts. https://www.mirror.co.uk/3am/us-celebrity-news/taylor-swift-fans-fume-spotify-28293255

[110] Bonus tracks, new video, a Spotify crash: Swift's 'Midnights' is full of surprises. Nardine Saad https://www.latimes.com/entertainment-arts/music/story/2022-10-21/taylor-swift-midnights-bonus-tracks-anti-hero-video-spotify

[111] Kylie Jenner helps to wipe $1bn from Snapchat with tweet over redesign woes. Alex Hern. https://www.theguardian.com/technology/2018/feb/22/snapchat-redesign-12m-signature-petition-social-media-app-kylie-jenner-celebrities

[112] Why most redesigns fail. Girish Rawat. https://www.freecodecamp.org/news/why-most-redesigns-fail-6ecaaf1b584e/

[113] Why Snapchat's re-redesign will fail and how to fix it. Josh Constine. https://techcrunch.com/2018/05/11/how-snapchat-should-work/

[114] Windows 8 — Disappointing Usability for Both Novice and Power. Jakob Nielsen Usershttps://www.nngroup.com/articles/windows-8-disappointing-usability/

[115] Usability expert finds Windows 8 on a PC confusing. Lisa Eadicicco. https://www.nbcnews.com/tech/gadgets/usability-expert-finds-windows-8-pc-confusing-flna954680

[116] The Windows 8 Disaster. Martin Irvine. https://blogs.commons.georgetown.edu/cctp-820-fall2017/2017/10/11/the-windows-8-disaster/

ABOUT THE AUTHOR

Delvis Echeverria, with over 15 years of experience in QA and Software Testing, has worked on complex projects across various industries such as Health, Financial, Field Services, Retail, IT, and Academic sectors in the US and Latin America. He holds a bachelor's degree in computer science and a master's degree in software quality. Delvis has been an esteemed Instructor and Assistant Professor, teaching Software Engineering, Databases, and Software Testing since 2007. He is a sought-after speaker for webinars and conferences. Currently, he resides and works as a Software QA Manager from the Sunshine State, Florida.

www.ingramcontent.com/pod-product-compliance
Lightning Source LLC
Chambersburg PA
CBHW071604270726
48661CB00018B/1243